"Are we witnessing the beginning of the end or are we seeing a new birth of history and of the Church? Will the collapse of institutions drag everything into chaos, or will it set free a profound new life in the world and in the Church?

"It is a difficult question to answer. But it is possible to say that a little insecurity is good for us, who are too used to dogmatism and vehement assertions. Above all it is good for us as Christians to lose a little of that self-assuredness which made us incapable of dialogue, which made us think that it was enough to be in the boat, which made us feel that faith was so firm in us that it could suffer no darkness whatsoever."

—CARLO CARRETTO

THE GOD WHO COMES

Carlo Carretto

TRANSLATED BY ROSE MARY HANCOCK

For Sale By Distributor
LIVING FLAME PRESS
Box 74 Locust Valley, N. Y. 11560

ORBIS BOOKS
MARYKNOLL   NEW YORK

Biblical citations are taken from
The New American Bible

THE GOD WHO COMES

Published by Pillar Books for Orbis Books

Paperback edition published January 1976

ISBN: 0-88344-164-0

Library of Congress Catalog Card Number: 73-89358

Originally published by Citta Nuova Editrice, Rome

Copyright © 1974 by Orbis Books

All Rights Reserved

Printed in the United States of America

ORBIS BOOKS
Maryknoll, New York 10545

CONTENTS

INTRODUCTION

Today, both the world and the Church have entered what is perhaps one of the most dramatic periods in all history.

The dimensions of our lives coincide with the dimensions of the whirling cosmos. The speed of change makes even a single day unstable. This speed forces man to question everything: as never before he feels the agent, even builder, of his own destiny, yet at the same time he feels himself to be almost an atom lost in the unmeasured galaxies.

In the minds and hearts of Christians yesterday, the Church was a rock of safety and stability. Now it has become an open arena for every kind of contest, profound or superficial. Clerics and bishops dispute openly, even angrily, and the average Christian grows frightened, lost among increasingly anonymous and strangely restless crowds.

Many people take refuge in inaction and isolation. Many take up any kind of hobby just to pass the time. Others assume the role of prophet, even though they have nothing to prophesy. And many, finding no other solution, close themselves off in fond memories of the past, dreaming of Latin liturgies, fervent processions, and blind obedience. And, of course, everyone does his best to get just one drop of pleasure out of life (even amid eloquent speeches on the Third World) contributing to a civilization of material prosperity, sex, drugs—the permissive society, a decadent civilization.

It is as though a cyclone or an earthquake had just passed, not destroying the house completely, but leaving us insecure. We are discovering the cracks, and there is an undefined sadness in our hearts.

We have aged centuries in a few years, and even our recent spiritual past seems far, far away. What is most distant is our sureness, our stability, our dogmatism.

The best metaphor for our world of today is an astronaut speeding through the cosmos, but with his life-supporting capsule pierced by a meteorite fragment. But the Church resembles Mary and Joseph traveling from Egypt to Nazareth on a donkey, holding in their arms the weakness and poverty of the Child Jesus: God incarnate.

But is this situation wholly bad? Is there not a good root, a life-giving principle, in today's torment and crisis? Can we draw something constructive from the ruins of our past? In short, are we witnessing the beginning of the end or are we seeing a new birth of history and of the Church? Will the collapse of institutions drag everything into chaos, or will it set free a profound new life in the world and in the Church?

It is a difficult question to answer. But it is possible to say that a little insecurity is good for us, who are too used to dogmatism and vehement assertions. Above all it is good for us as Christians to lose a little of that self-assuredness which made us incapable of dialogue, which made us think that it was enough to be in the boat, which made us feel that faith was so firm in us that it could suffer no darkness whatsoever.

And, as Christians, it is good for us to become humbler, smaller, less defensive: not to consider any longer others as "others," not to boast of the Resurrection and triumph of Christ without accepting the tremendous reality of His Crucifixion and death in us.

Another thing is good for us, turning us into adults, even if it is bitter for many: the hour of truth is being sounded with greater strength.

It sounds for every man.

No one can hide any longer behind screens of preconceived ideas and ready-made laws, constituted order and venerable traditions.

Everything is being questioned, rethought, judged in the light of new awareness and a more adult faith. Bread is bread and must be given to everyone; the Pope is the Pope, not "God on earth"; faith is faith, and not sentiment or reason; the common good is the common good, not the interests of the few; obedience is obedience, not the tyranny of authorities and the take-a-chance attitude of subjects; the Church is the Church, not a group of untouchables.

Above all we have a definite decision we must take, a meeting we must seek, a faith we must strengthen: the rediscovery of a personal God. At a certain moment every one of us must discover the God of Abraham, the God of Moses, the God of Elijah, the God of the gospel. For too long authentic faith in a personal God has dried up in individual souls, screened or hidden by the Church.

We believed in the Church and the Church believed in God; we entrusted ourselves to the Church and the Church spoke to God. We were like children from whom the mother had removed the difficult burden of presenting ourselves naked before the majesty of the Father.

So, to many, the Church substituted for Christ and pious muttering took the place of personal contemplation of the Transcendent.

In my youth it was common to hear people with the best intentions say, "I'm consecrating myself to the Church," "I'm consecrating myself to Catholic Action," "I'm consecrating myself to the Catholic University," "I'm consecrating myself to my bishop;" they did not realize that one could only consecrate oneself to God, to God alone.

The screen of the Church and "religious" things took up nearly all the space in our minds and souls. Now the screen has fallen (or rather, become more transparent through our awareness of a deeper sense of values). We feel like termites which, thrust out of their habitual darkness, wriggle under the sunlight, crying out their vulnerability to the light.

Yes, we felt unable to speak directly to God, to talk to Him without interpreters. So we feel alone amid the broken-down walls of an institution we ourselves caused to fall.

Today many people go around terrified amid the ruins of their spiritual past. They no longer feel any Presence.

How many, once they have forgotten the formulas which they used as children, no longer know how to pray?

And . . . why pray if you don't feel the presence of Him who dries our tears (cf. Ps. 56:9)?

And what if this Presence does not exist? The question is full of anguish for many.

Beyond doubt, this is the true nature of today's crisis.

The downfall of what is sacred, the unrelenting thrust of secularization have laid bare the altars of our faith and wiped out the "signs" which in one way or another helped us to enter into the "Invisible" and showed us His presence. Now, many wander sadly round this temple of the fallen myths. They go right up to the most intimate part of it, the Holy of Holies, the Tabernacle, and begin to wonder, "Is it empty? Is His Presence still there?"

The reply does not come quickly or easily when, for so long, we have been unused to the life of faith, satisfied with culture, memories, vague sentiment.

It is not easy, distracted as we are, to remain still before the Eucharistic Absolute, the real summation of all the mysteries of faith, the living, honored sign of the presence of God among us.

It is easier to circle round outside, seeking another form of God's presence in the world.

The most excellent persons, the most generous, the most full of life, seek out the man of today and say "Here is His presence! Man is God's presence on earth!" But perhaps those words of Jesus—"Where two or three are gathered in my name, there am I in their midst" (Matt. 18:20), or ". . . as often as you did

11

it for one of my least brothers, you did it for me" (Matt. 25:40)—are never the true gospel for those religious souls who seek spirituality for today.

It is interesting to see this phenomenal discovery of the depths of mankind! This thirst to free man from slavery, ignorance, hunger.

Certainly this discovery is the great hope and strength of today; or rather it is the religion of those who no longer believe, or have difficulty in believing, in a transcendent God.

A friend said to me: "Don't ask me to waste time praying. Don't ask me to look for God in the solitude of your desert. For me, God is in man, and I will search for rapport with Him by serving man.

What can I reply? "Please God, may you succeed! Please God, may you be capable of so much!

"You say this to me because you do not yet know man, you do not yet know your weakness in serving man! Keeping an attitude of love and service before the tabernacle of man when you have discovered his egoism, arrogance, and capacity for betrayal, is a frightening and demanding task."

Serving man is at once very easy and very difficult.

It is easier when you are young and bound to man by optimism or sentiment or nature or interest. It is more difficult when you have been abandoned and rejected by everyone, as happened to Jesus on the night of His betrayal. Man is not just the nice brother or interesting sister of your group; he is Judas, the capitalist, the egoist, the soldier who tortures you; the racist who despises you, the smug cleric who is so sure of his own perfection.

Man is man, all men: saint or sinner, American or

Chinese, Arab or Jew, white or black, cleric or anti-cleric.

If, without Christ, without the personal help of God, it was possible for man to love and serve man to the uttermost, up to the final sacrifice of himself, the Incarnation would have been unnecessary.

No man is capable of so much. Sooner or later he will discover within himself how heroic it is to love, how immature his own love is; how great a need he has for a "Power from on high" and divine comfort to resist the temptation of hating everybody and escaping into a cave to live out his own isolation.

Yes, I'm saying this bluntly because I have experience of it: only God can help us to love man, only Christ can teach us this difficult lesson.

But the problem does not truly lie here.

The true problem is this: is God an autonomous presence before you, like you before your friend, the bridegroom before the bride, the Son before the Father? Or is He present only in things and thus in the greatest and most interesting thing, man?

Can you meet God as a person on your road and prostrate yourself before Him as did Moses before the burning bush? Can you feel His caress as did Elias on Mount Oreb? Can you experience His presence in the dark intimacy of the temple as did the prophets?

In short, is God the God of transcendence, and thus the God of prayer, the God of what lies beyond things, or is He only the God of immanence, revealing Himself in the evolution of matter, in the dynamics of history, in the promise to free mankind?

This is the real problem of today, as always, and it is

13

a problem of choice: action or prayer, revolution or contemplation—without taking into account the truism that sin is not what we do, but what we omit doing.

Truth is always a synthesis of opposites, and it is so difficult to reach. It is easier, much easier, to let ourselves be carried on by the force of error that pushes us furiously, joyfully to the extremes of dilemma, causing us to forget "the other aspect of things." But in so acting, we build on emptiness, and we do not find peace.

We are without peace!

In the Gospel there is a hard saying of Jesus that should be remembered when we speak of action: "for apart from me you can do nothing" (John 15:5).

Who is this Jesus who has the courage to say to men of all time "apart from me you can do nothing"? Is He one of the many great persons who lived in time, disappeared with death, and are now present to men, if at all, in their teachings? Or is He, as Peter calls Him, under the inspiration of the Spirit, "the Son of the living God" (Matt. 16:16)?

And if He is living, how does He come to me, who am alive?

Does He come to me as a cloud or as a person?

Does He come to me as a person, or does He come to me through His words, spoken two thousand years ago and transmitted by the Evangelists in the gospels?

Here is the problem.

The Church believes and I believe that Jesus is the Son of the living God; that before His incarnation, He was alive as the Word of God; that after His death and

14

resurrection He remains alive, with His covenant—or marriage—with mankind accomplished.

God wanted a covenant with mankind: this covenant is both the content and the goal of the whole plan of salvation. But a covenant must be made between the living, not the dead, and between persons, not concepts or symbols.

If the truth is that God, in His mercy, has desired an alliance with me, He must enter upon my road, where I can meet Him.

Personal prayer is the meeting place between the Eternal One and me; the Blessed Sacrament is the visible sign of my covenant with Him.

This is why I believe in personal prayer, and why every day I wait to meet Him in the Eucharist. To pray means to wait for the God who comes.

Every prayer-filled day sees a meeting with the God who comes; every night which we faithfully put at His disposal is full of His presence.

And His coming and His presence are not only the result of our waiting or a prize for our efforts: they are His decision, based on His love freely poured out.

His coming is bound to His promise, not to our works or virtue. We have not earned the meeting with God because we have served Him faithfully in our brethren, or because we have heaped up such a pile of virtue as to shine before Heaven.

God is thrust onward by His love, not attracted by our beauty. He comes even in moments when we have done everything wrong, when we have done nothing . . . when we have sinned.

It was pride that made people think that the coming of the Messiah would be in virtue of the Law and not

15

of the Promise. Today, it is still pride that makes one think God's coming in prayer is the fruit of man's efforts and not a gift of God's love.

That is why those who think they can find God solely by serving their fellow men are unconsciously motivated by pride. They entrust the meeting to the fruit of their own efforts.

What about the prostitutes and publicans upon this road? They have done nothing for the service of their fellows; on the contrary. And yet, as the gospel says, they have met Christ and believed in Him.

We, too, want to meet Him, just as we are, beyond ourselves, beyond our sins and our virtues.

We want to meet Him because He is God, and we cannot live without God.

We want to meet Him because He is light, and we cannot walk without light.

We want to meet Him because He is love, and there is no joy without love.

And we want to meet Him because by doing so we shall strengthen the covenant He has offered us. Everything else will come out right if Christians will remember their covenant with the Eternal One.

If there is a crisis in the Church, it is a crisis of Christians—of their faith, of their prayer, of their contemplation.

When each Christian has strenghtened his faith in the living God, he will find it easy to take to the road again. When the vital, personal relationship with Christ has been renewed, it will be easy to renew a vital, personal relationship with the Church. Not before.

The Second Vatican Council, possibly the most extraordinary religious event of our time, was the manifestation of the freshness and vitality of the Church. It was a moment of deep joy for those who were "waiting," a time of wonderful awareness of the mystery of the Church and its presence in the world. But it was useless for those who had lost their faith, and turned away from the ever-flowing spring of man's converse with the Eternal One.

The entire bible closes with an invocation, which St. John puts into the mouth of the bride. It is a summing up of all the impassioned prayers to Heaven after the departure of Christ from earth: "Come, Lord Jesus" (Rev. 22:20).

What is the meaning of this cry to Jesus who once lived among us but disappeared physically from our history after His death, resurrection, and ascension?

All Christians know. It is a crying out for the return of Christ in his final manifestation. His Second Coming will close history and introduce the Messianic era, the eternal feast of heaven.

But it would be too cruel if we simply had to wait for the "Last Day," if the Christian life could have no contact with the Person of Christ until the end of the world!

The Kingdom of God will come on the Last Day, but it has also already come, and is "in us." The return of Christ, which will take place with the thunder of the Apocalypse, also occurs every day, every evening, every night when I open my heart to Him, and search for Him in the Sacrament and in prayer.

The bride may meet the bridegroom whenever she

wishes. The Christ of faith is always coming to visit His bride, and He comes in person.

That is why the meeting is real, both in the Sacrament and in prayer.

By prayer I mean waiting for "the God who comes." And this "coming" means not waiting outside on the doorstep but entering in.

While she is waiting for the Messianic feast, of which the Eucharist is the proclamation, the bride is admitted to the "little feast of wisdom," which is contemplation.

A passage from Proverbs says: "Wisdom has built her house, she has set up her seven columns. She has dressed her meat, mixed her wine" (Prov. 9:1-2).

Christ replies to our vigilant faith with His coming. "I go away for a while, and I come back to you" (John 14:28), He said at the Last Supper.

And so he comes back to remain in intimacy with us and accompany us through history.

It is said that the spirituality of man on earth is the spirituality of Exodus, of the long journey which stretches from the freedom up from slavery to the joys of the Promised Land, possessed and enjoyed for ever.

Well, on the march through the desert, God did not send His people emptiness and solitude but the surety of His Presence, proclaimed by the cloud above the Tabernacle.

This was the sign of the living Presence of Yahweh. But it was also the proclamation of a much closer and more loving Presence which Christ was to bring about in the new covenant with mankind. In the first covenant God used words and symbols to convince man; in the second, He used a chalice of blood, "the cup of the blood of Jesus shed for all of us."

Would He who tells me of His love by giving me His blood stay far from me? To doubt the presence of Jesus in my life is lack of faith. And it is lack of faith to think that He who gives me His sacrificial chalice to drink does not at the same time give me His presence and His friendship.

And that is why once more I lift up the chalice of his covenant, full of the blood of my God, and inebriated with Him, I cry out in all faith, "Come, Lord Jesus."

"Come, Lord Jesus!"
(Rev. 22:20)

PART I

God has always been coming. He came in the creation of light, and he came yet more in Adam. He came in Abraham but was to come more fully in Moses. He came in Elijah, but was to come even more fully in Jesus. The God who comes takes part in the procession of time. With history He localizes Himself in the geography of the cosmos, in the consciousness of man, and in the Person of Christ. He has come and has yet to come.

CHAPTER I

". . . they heard the sound of the Lord God moving about in the garden in the cool of the day" (Gen. 3:8).

God is always coming, and we, like Adam, hear His footsteps.

God is always coming because He is life, and life has the unbridled force of creation.

God comes because He is light, and light may not remain hidden.

God comes because He is love, and love needs to give of itself. God has always been coming; God is always coming.

This evening, as I gazed at the extraordinary desert sky, I saw the heavenly body farthest from the earth and still visible to the naked eye: the nebula of Andromeda. It appeared as a pale, lentil-shaped light between the geometric regularity of Cassiopeia and the Pleiades' incomparable diamond. The light of that tiny lentil is not the light of today; it is from a million years ago.

This evening I saw backwards a million years, ten thousand centuries.

The pale light of the nebula, which reached my eye this evening, left there a million years ago at the speed of 187,000 miles per second. From that time, and doubtless from before then, God had been coming to meet me.

But Andromeda is only the nearest galaxy to ours; by now astronomers are used to calculating distances in the tens of thousands of light years which separate us from the many other galaxies lost in space.

It is a long time since God set out to come to me, a time I was not yet born. Neither had the sun nor the moon nor the earth nor my history nor my problems been born.

I am not a scholar, but those who are tell us that the earth beneath our feet came into being two billion years ago. Then it was prepared for man by the different geological eras during which God's creativity was expressed in all its power and gentleness: "evening came, and morning followed" (Gen. 1:5).

But between one morning and another, one evening and another . . . how much time!

Precambrian: one billion five hundred million years!

Primary: Four hundred million years.

Tertiary: Fifty million years!

And finally the Quaternary, with the presence of man, which began one million years ago.

Any small errors in calculation must be excused. They should be laid to the weakness of our eyesight rather than to the precision of evolution; creation was not preoccupied with counting, but with loving, and the precision of love is not the same as the precision of mathematics.

Anyway, I like looking at the sky and the earth. I don't feel I'm wasting time.

When I come to pray in the desert, I prepare my prayer by contemplating things. I think the Lord put things there just for that.

When I was younger and more impatient I used to get bored when the junior scouts opened their tents and gazed curiously and affectionately at the woods and at the tiny animals under the yellowing leaves. It seemed a waste of time. I would have preferred to have them taught catechism in some church.

I was immature and did not understand that the best catechism is to fix our eyes on created things, because through things God begins to speak to us.

It may be, through teaching catechism to bored students sitting on benches, teaching abbreviated formulas and intellectual summaries, that we have destroyed everything, leaving them sad and absent before the mystery of God.

Today, so many years later, how I should like to replace a catechism lesson with a walk in the fields, offering to a boy who lives buried in the inhuman cemetery of the city, the wonderful discovery of a sparrow's nest!

For is not wonder the first, unconscious meeting with mystery? Does not wonder give birth to the first prayer? Does not the power to contemplate involve first the power to be awed?

When I prepare my prayer, I fix my eyes on the earth and sky; even further, I immerse myself in them.

Before beginning my dialogue with God, I look round at the bit of earth where He wants me to be. It is no waste of time to wander about looking at things, touching them, contemplating them. In fact, it is necessary to go further: one must *live* things.

Don't laugh when I tell you that I have made a discovery about "living things." It consists of entering into the game of creation and is the most marvelously simple way of meeting the Creator.

I prepare myself for the game by stripping down to the greatest possible sense of freedom.

For example, if I came down here to the desert in good clothes, I'd immediately feel a slave to them. I'd have the usual fear of getting dirty or losing the crease in my trousers. No, I come in old rags so that I can roll in the sand every time the joy of God takes hold of me.

If I brought with me all kinds of mechanical and electrical gadgets, I should lose the joy of gathering wood in the *oued* and seeing the living flame between the two stones, simple and true, like creation.

How wonderful to make supper in a smokey black saucepan which can then be cast aside to stand contentedly in a silent corner, like the old ladies of time past.

But I must go still further to enter into a serious game of nature. I must accept the wind, the sand, the night's cold, the day's heat, the discomforts, poor health, disappointments, as speeches made by God to teach me poverty and patience, not as provocations for useless complaining.

Above all, I must turn backward in time and approach the origin of things. Then matter was more visible than machines, and the beauty of sunsets closer than the gadgets of a consumer society.

Yes, I try to enter into things, like the primitive men who lived in nature and with nature, who did not even pose themselves the problem of God's existence. They did not need to demonstrate it because they could feel it. God was there and they heard Him "moving in the garden in the cool of the day" (Gen. 3:8).

God's presence is obvious to anyone who can hear His footsteps.

Yes, obvious. God's existence is obvious. But it is obvious only to the man who is simple, good, true. And we, unfortunately, are no longer simple, good, or true: we are sinners.

God is not obvious to the sinner. Or at least, He is and He isn't. This God who both is and is not obvious in nature, I call the God of parable.

Everything is His parable, but faced with a parable I feel perplexed. I see and I don't see; I understand, and I don't understand. Jesus Himself, continuing the method of nature in His first revelation to man, spoke in parables and explained why: "I use parables because they look but do not see, they listen but do not hear or understand" (Matt. 13:13).

The God of parables is not yet the God of faith, just as the man of nature is not yet the man of grace. A new intervention from God is needed, a new creation must establish the new relationship, which is part of the history of salvation. When this has not yet begun, man hears in creation "the sound of the Lord God moving about in the garden" and, like Adam, flees from His

29

presence, and hides "among the trees of the garden" (Gen. 3:8).

Why does he run away? Because, without his old innocence, he is afraid to stand before God. Because, with his former vision lost, he can no longer see Him as He is.

Here is the real difficulty men of all time have in seeing God in creation. They are no longer simple and no longer true; the name for their condition is sin.

If a man is to prepare himself for faith, he must free himself from its real obstacle, sin. "Unless you change and become like little children, you will not enter the kingdom of Heaven" (Matt. 18:3), Jesus says forcefully. And becoming like little children means becoming transparent, good, true.

Every step a man takes to free himself from lies, baseness, violence, egoism, and pride, is a step towards the vision of God. Every effort to live the truth, to do good, to respect life is an early preparation for the coming of the Light. It is certain that the Light will come, driven only by the love of God. It is equally certain that it can be seen by anyone who has renounced darkness.

Listen to the prologue of the Gospel of St. John. With what strength he affirms this truth about the coming light and about man's power not to accept it!

> *In the beginning was the Word;*
> *the Word was in God's presence,*
> *and the Word was God.*
> *He was present to God in the beginning.*
> *Through him all things came into being,*
> *and apart from him nothing came to be.*

30

Whatever came to be in him, found life,
life for the light of men.
The light shines on in the darkness,
a darkness that did not overcome it.

There was a man named John sent by God, who came as a witness to testify to the light, so that through him all men might believe but only to testify to the light, for he himself was not the light.
The real light which gives light to every man was coming into the world.

He was in the world,
and through him the world was made,
yet the world did not know who he was.
To his own he came,
yet his own did not accept him.

(John 1:1-11)

So, we can refuse to accept the light or fail to want it. This is our real drama. Sometimes we give the impression of wanting to search for God; we even say we do. But in reality we don't want to be bothered; we don't want to make the necessary renunciations.

We say we want faith, but we don't want to open our purses to the poor. We claim we are looking for Christ, but we make no effort to change our lives, even though we can see how mistaken they are.

I feel I must give the lie to any man who says, "I'm looking for God, but I can't find him!" Let him try to do everything in the truth, free from the demon of pride and the suffering density of egoism. Let every trace of racism be rooted out, let every man be welcomed as a brother, and . . . you will see, you will see!

Live *love*. Act *truth*. Honor *life*. And it will be God within you whom you live, act, and honor. God will not come to you because you have become "good." He was already there. He has always been coming and always is coming. But now you can see Him because you have purified your eyes, softened your heart, and stooped down.

Remember! He was already there, He was already there, He was already there! The only difficulty was that you were unable to see Him.

Now you identify love and light and life more and more with Him. You see Him even if He is still veiled and expressed in the mysterious parable of created things.

CHAPTER II

"The Lord said to Abram, 'Leave your country.' " (Gen. 12:1)

The God of parables, however much He may occupy a man's life, is still very far from holding his deep interest. He is still a God who shows Himself through the veil of symbols. He sends a postcard from far off, a drawing, a picture, a calling-card. He is a God you think of as "clothed with majesty and glory" (Ps. 104:1) and who travels "on the wings of the wind" (Ps. 104:3).

He is a God who comes and goes in your existence. He appears and disappears, and you can never localize Him or catch hold of Him.

All in all, He is a God who is distant from you, even if He seems very close at times. It is as though He has decided not to get caught by you, or as though you are not yet ready to get caught by Him.

He is still hidden in an untold story, an unopened seed.

Then a great moment arrives, a transition, an immense jump in quality, something really new. The hour has come.

It is the hour of God; it is the fullness of time. *It is a passage to the God of faith.*

The God of parables was the God who *seemed* to be. The God of faith is the God who *is*.

He no longer shows Himself as a symbol, an image, a piece of reasoning, a thing of beauty, an aesthetic concept, a number, a space, or feeling. He shows Himself as a person. This God-who-is speaks: "The Lord said to Abram, 'Leave your country' " (Gen. 12:1).

It is a radical passage, even if foreordained since time began by God's love for man. With Abram, a new era begins in the history of mankind, an era of men of faith, of men to whom God has given power to believe in the God who *is*.

The relationship between the creature and the Creator becomes close. It becomes awareness, dialogue, prayer, friendship: "Shall I hide from Abram what I am about to do?" (Gen. 18:17).

It becomes relevation and command: "Look up at the sky and count the stars if you can. Just so . . . shall your descendents be" (Gen. 15:5).

When I pray, I am no longer before the God of parables, but the God of my faith. I pray to *Somebody*, I speak with *Someone*.

The situation is completely changed. The God of philosophy, the God of reason, the God of parables has given place to the God of faith, and the God of faith is before me as Father, before me as Christ, before me as Spirit—always as a Person.

My poor human personality has finally found the

34

"Other" with whom it may speak. The "Other" is God in His being, His truth, His love.

The passage to faith is radical, absolute; only God is capable of starting it, carrying it through, controlling it. That is why theologians say that faith is a God-given gift.

But that is always true of everything. What is not a God-given gift?

Even in evolution, in the moment of passage, when an inferior form of life becomes a "homo sapiens," the Creator Spirit is present to blow gently into it a new reality so that man is no longer just any animal: he is a man.

"The Lord God formed man out of the clay of the ground and blew into his nostrils the breath of life, and so man became a living being" (Gen. 2:7).

Yes, in the fullness of the history of living creatures on earth, in the fullness of God's love, a sheath of nerves and muscles and a handful of gray matter became conscious man. And now that man becomes a man who believes; he is beginning a history which is to go far, eventually to the perfect intimacy of creature with Creator.

Faith is a gift from God, just as life is. And the passage of faith is a gift from God. God holds this gift in His hand and offers it when He wills, when the right hour has come. The hour of love is always His.

We should meditate more on a saying of Jesus in order to understand that *everything* is in His hand, not ours: "No one can come to me, unless the Father who sent me draws him" (John 6:44).

He truly has to attract us to begin the process of

35

transformation and union. It all must begin with the magnetic force of the Father's love.

The Father attracts me, calls me, and I reply. Thus faith is born in me and is put into movement within me like a living seed.

It is not enough for faith to be born and placed inside the living foetus of a child's soul at baptism. Faith must develop, move, be nourished. This is partly my responsibility.

If I do not respond to the word of God, faith remains aborted inside me. If I do not keep it active with zeal and the exercise of virtue, it remains immature and weak, like the limbs of a paralytic. If I do not feed it with the food of union with God it becomes a ghostly shadow, more likely to frighten the inhabitants of the house than to bring gladness to the human community through its joyful presence.

By faith man has become aware of the "Other." The friend has found his Friend; the betrothed has gazed on her Loved One; the son has become acquainted with his Father.

Thus begins the relationship; faith, the God-given possibility of this living, conscious relationship with Him.

When I believe, I speak with God. When I believe, I listen to God. When I believe, I see God.

The life of faith is the most extraordinary thing that exists on earth; it casts into shadow the gifts we received formerly, just as the gift of becoming man cast into shadow the gift of being born to light.

With faith I become a participant in God's life, entering a new orbit, the orbit of God. With faith I pass through the heavens, travel in the invisible, conquer the strength of my human nature, overcome my weakness, become a son of God.

This is so extraordinary that there is no limit to its grandeur or the possibilities of its development. Faith enables me to conquer fear, to overcome death. It is invincible. St. John says, "the power that has conquered the world is this faith of ours" (I John 5:4).

Indeed, what is left to fear if God is my Father? What possibility can worry me, if I conclude with the most extraordinary possiblity that can be imagined: eternal life? The fullness of the Kingdom? The resurrection of the dead? The Agape of all redeemed men with God Himself at the table?

Now with faith I know what to believe, what to want, what to do. With faith I become "someone," called by name by God Himself, given my mandate by God Himself.

In fact, my vocation is born with faith: "The Lord God said to Abram, "Leave your country" (Gen. 12:1).

And with Abram, I, too, am leaving my old country and traveling towards the Promised Land, which is God Himself.

CHAPTER III

"God put Abraham to the test" (Gen. 22:1).

Early on we understand that faith is a risk; much later we learn the price of this risk.

All God's patience is devoted to difficult pupils like ourselves, because He wants us to take on this risk!

But it is not only a case of being difficult pupils. It is the rub of getting down seriously to marching along one of the most rugged paths in existence.

I do not believe there is a more difficult task in the world than living on faith, hope, and love! We have to make a leap into the darkness or, more precisely, into the Invisible.

It is not easy. I have been used to it for a long time, and yet I tremble when a new leap is proposed by the presence of God in my conscience.

It is like pain, or, rather death. You never become accustomed to it.

You find yourself in front of a dark well and you

hear the order, "Close your eyes and jump in." That isn't easy for anyone.

Perhaps hope can help you. "I, the Lord, am your God who brought you out of the land of Egypt" (Deut. 5:6). . . . I am with you. . . . I am with you. . . . Perhaps memory can come to your aid, the experience of countless other leaps in your life in which you have come to no harm. On the contrary, you have had the immense joy of that moment of experiencing God's presence. But the knowledge that you must begin again fills you with fear.

It is useless to hide it. Faith is a trial, a tremendous trial, like death itself, and no one can get us out of it, not even God Himself.

I think I can truthfully say that God has no greater interest on our behalf than to see us plunged in this act of faith. He is like a lover watching anxiously from the window for the arrival of His beloved.

He is like a father who enjoys watching His son run searching through the crowds towards Him.

For we must not forget that faith is not separate from love. At bottom it is the proof of love; I should call it the first proof.

"But without faith it is impossible to please Him" (Heb. 11:6).

The first proof of love is to believe in the One loved.

The first proof of love is to believe in His presence.

If I do not believe in His presence, how can I speak with Him?

Having faith means believing that He is there before me, with all His love, all His omnipotence.

Having faith means believing that He fills all space, that no leap can cast me out from His arms. Having faith means believing that He knows everything, that before I arrive He runs through the infinitely complicated plan of my existence all the way to its conclusion, like an ever new problem solved by his infinite love: my final entry into His Kingdom.

Believing in God means all this and still more.

Only very late do we learn the price of the risk of believing, because only very late do we face up to the idea of death.

This is what is difficult: believing truly means dying. Dying to everything: to our reasoning, to our plans, to our past, to our childhood dreams, to our attachment to earth, and sometimes even to the sunlight, as at the moment of our physical death.

That is why faith is so difficult. It is so difficult to hear from Jesus a cry of anguish for us and our difficulties in believing, "Oh, if only you could believe!"

Because not even He can take our place in the leap of Faith; it is up to us. It *is* like dying! It is up to us, and no one is able to take our place.

This mature act of faith is terribly, uniquely personal. Its risk involves us down to the core; the truest and greatest prototype of this act of faith that we, as the People of God, possess is the biblical account of the trial of Abraham. "God said, 'Take your son Isaac, your only one whom you love, and go to the land of Moriah. There you shall offer him up as a holocaust on a height that I will point out to you'" (Gen. 22:2).

That is a leap of pure faith proposed to Abraham!

It is a personal act, and it is an act of death.

Without love it is impossible to understand such a proposal; on the contrary, it is scandalous.

But for anyone who loves?

40

Seeing God wrapt round the colossal figure of this patriarch, alone in the desert beside his tent . . . no, that is no scandal, but quite the contrary.

God wants to communicate with the depths of Abraham's being and tear him from himself and his involvement with his own problems, which are like self-centered possessions; He wants to make this creature of His "more His," this man who is destined not for the tents of earth, but for those of Heaven. So God asks of him an absurd trial, as love is absurd for anyone who does not live it, but as true and relentless as love for anyone who possesses it. " 'Take your son . . .' " (Gen. 22:2).

I believe that at dawn that morning the angels from every corner of Heaven were busy preparing the mountain on which a man was about to carry out such a tragic and radical rite of love!

I believe that at sunrise on that eastern morning the space around Abraham was quilted by the invisible eyes of all who had died before him, wanting to see what the ending would be!

What a drama was in the poor heart of that man! God had asked the supreme sacrifice. If Abraham had had to turn the knife on himself it would have been easier!

An act of pure faith is the death of what we love most so it may be offered to the loved one because only love is stronger than death.

Set me as a seal on your heart,
as a seal on your arm;
For stern as death is love
. . . .

41

Deep waters cannot quench love,
nor floods sweep it away.

(Sg. of Sg. 8:6-7)

No, the floods of thought and reasoning before the absurdity of the request, the floods of emotion before the affection of Isaac cannot quench in Abraham's heart the act of love which binds him to his God, his "beloved above everything," the apex of all values.

God is God, and Abraham runs the risk right to the end.

God is God and He takes up all rational space and also that which man thinks is irrational.

God is God, and He puts everything right in His love for His creature. He will not permit him to come to harm in his act of loving Him.

Faith is not separated from love and hope!

At the ultimate moment of trial, when man tries to pierce the invisible with the sharpened spear of every possibility he can find, he realizes that the three theological virtues—faith, hope, and charity—are really only one, and they have such a power of penetration that they could disrupt the entire universe.

On Mount Moriah, in the trial of Abraham, man embraced God as never before. The experience of this embrace reverberates through the religious history of the world as an epic of a love greater than man's endless frailty.

Not for nothing does this tragic rite of love conclude with an extraordinary promise from God.

" 'I swear by myself, declares the Lord, that because you acted as you did in not withholding from me your beloved son, I will bless you abundantly and make your descendants as countless as the stars of the sky and the sands of the seashore; your descendants shall take possession of the gates of their enemies, and in your descendants all the nations of the earth shall find blessing—all this because you obeyed my command.' " (Gen. 22:16-18)

I do not know whether in my life I shall be presented with such a hard act of faith as Abraham was. I hope not, for I am small and weak.

But I know I shall be presented with one of the same kind: *my death.*

That is why I said the price of the risk of faith is death itself. It is personal. It is mine.

It makes me smile to hear the nonsense talked by those who try to distract me from this real problem. It is I who have to die. And dying is a leap into the dark which I have to get used to little by little.

Every act of faith I make in my life is training for this hard passage. Reasoning certainly does not solve the problem. Neither does the thought that Christianity is an organ of social justice and the liberation of oppressed peoples. This distribution of my land to the poor, this freedom of peoples to which I have contributed with all my energy are only the beginning. They are the entrance visa to a more radical distribution and a more complete liberation which death imposes on me.

At the very moment of my death I must carry out an action which is terribly irrational for anyone who has seen only the earth, terribly painful for anyone still attached to it, terribly scandalous for anyone who believes so little in the Absolute that he remains grounded and petrified with fear.

43

But I hope it will not be so for me.

I hope not, because I cling onto faith as the only table of salvation.

I hope not, because as long as I have breath in me, night and day, I sharpen my weapons for the final agony.

I hope not, because I say every hour, " 'I do believe! Help my lack of trust!' " (Mark 9:24).

How everything changes when I have faith!

Indeed, to die in faith is to carry out the highest act of love possible.

To plunge forward, head held high, "into the darkness," with the certainty of throwing myself into God's arms, is truly to render a service of love worthy of Him.

To pass with faith through the wall of the Invisible into His presence will be the greatest victory of my life and my dearest reply to His Fatherly heart.

CHAPTER IV

God called . . . "Moses! Moses!"
He answered, "Here I am." (Exod. 3:4)

The God of faith is not a God who is silent, a God who is inactive, a God who is not present to us.

To you who are a person, He is a person; to you who have life, He is life; to you who have love, He is love. He is the "Other" who is searching for you.

He has always been searching for you.

And you, too, are looking for the "Other," even when—and it often happens—you feel you are doing something quite different.

In the end everything we do on this earth is pushed on solely by this search for the "Other." We search for Him first in things. Then in creatures, with ever more intimate relationships. Finally, in the maturity of faith, the "Other" shows Himself to us as a transcendent and autonomous presence, detached from things and creatures, beyond creation: the Absolute.

I can never insist enough that this beginning of the

life of faith is governed by God himself. It is His gift, and we cannot anticipate it by a single instant, however many mountains of virtue we may heap up.

It is a freely given gift.

God comes like the sun in the morning—when it is time.

We must assume an attitude of waiting, accepting the fact that we are creatures and not creator.

We must do this because it is not our right to do anything else; the initiative is God's, not man's. Man is able to initiate nothing; he is able only to accept.

If God does not call, no calling takes place. If God does not come, there is no history! History is the coming of God to man, and the way in which man replies.

Only God created the heavens and the earth; only God can create history. Man carries it out through his response, but the inspiration, the design, and the strength to carry it out come from Him.

In short, He is what creates, and we creatures are in an act of becoming.

Sin, any kind of sin at all, is simply our exclusion of Him.

And sin is so easy! Perhaps because He "is hidden" (Isa. 45:15)? Or perhaps because our eyes are not clear, and our hearts are not pure?

Many people today do not exclude Him completely, but they identify Him with man, or with the freeing of humanity, or with history, or with just everything.

Things may seem that way, but they are not.

If I say with Teilhard de Chardin, "God is on the point of my pencil, on the point of my plough," I mean that between the inspiration of an action and its being carried through, between the vocation and the history of each of us, there must be the least possible space.

"Take out the space," they tell me, "And we can agree."

"No," I maintain. "Between Him and me there is always a space, even if only the thickness of the placenta in which I am enfolded like a foetus in his womb."

I am I, and He is He.

I am son, and He is Father.

I am one who waits, and He is the One who comes.

I am one who replies, and He is the One who calls.

In fact: "God called . . . 'Moses! Moses.' He answered, 'Here I am.' " (Exod. 3:4).

It is strange how many Christians today, although they diligently bend over their bibles, find difficulty in discovering and living the "personalism" of God. The God of the bible leaves no doubt about this point. He is always a personal God.

He is the God of Abraham, of Isaac, of Jacob. He is the God of Jesus. He is the God who commands, who reproves, who caresses. He is a voice which speaks, an ear which listens, an eye which sees.

Everyone agrees that the spirituality of man on earth is the spirituality of the Exodus. How is it possible, then, not to discover in the Exodus the two: God and man? God designing the plan of salvation for His people, and the people setting out on the march from Egypt? God calling Moses to the mountain to give him the tables of the Law, and Moses remaining on the mountain wrapped in the godhead of Yahweh? God warning against idolatry, and man falling into idolatry and worshipping the golden calf?

The two, always the two of them: man and God, I

and the "Other," the son and the Father, the bride and the Bridegroom, the friend and the Friend, the brother and the Brother.

Presence!

Dialogue!

Prayer!

Or perhaps, because to experience His presence is demanding, I must conclude that He is not there?

Or perhaps, because I have become deaf and dumb, I must declare that dialogue between Him and me does not exist?

Or perhaps, because I have not prayed for years, I must convince myself that prayer is no use?

Certainly, when I make a decision or perform some action, I have the clear impression that it is I who decide and act. But I must not assume too easily that there was no inspiration or that the strength to carry these things out came from me and me alone.

It takes a long time to distinguish within ourselves between the two things, the two moments: the inspiration and the reply, grace and faith. But the time comes, and then we are convinced that there is nothing in us that is not from God.

Everything comes from Him; everything is born of Him; everything is created by Him.

It is for us to accept, to follow through, to contemplate.

Creativity is God's.

Collaboration is ours.

The call is God's.

The reply is ours.

And apart from the drama of there being two of us, what is going to happen to that love which is the explanation of everything? Making love takes two, and they must be very close.

Anyone who does not feel God near him and has forgotten how to converse, to weep, to ask, to cry out is heading for sadness; that is the first sign of ruin.

No one can be fulfilled alone, never.

We always need something, someone, right on up to God, right on up to the fullness of the heavenly banquet where we shall all, all be in God.

Until that hour we shall not be truly fulfilled.

That is why we suffer on this earth. Suffering is a pulling, an agonizing struggle towards unity, and that is the fullness and bliss of having finally found the "Other."

God Himself, of whom we are the image, is not a God alone.

A God alone would be a solitary and not a God of love.

God is a Trinity because He is love. The Trinity of God is the fullness of love, of communication, of giving.

In the Gospel Jesus continually refers to an "Other," whom He calls His Father, and His words should leave no doubt about the communication between the two divine Persons: " 'Doing the will of Him who sent me / and bringing His work to completion / is my food.' " (John 4:34); and again: " '. . . I have not come of Myself / I was sent by One who has the right to send.' " (John 7:28).

" '. . . I do nothing by Myself / I say only what the Father has taught me.' " (John 8:28); and again, more firmly, " 'The One who sent Me is with Me / He has not deserted Me / since I always do what pleases Him.' " (John 8:29).

Here is the nature and meaning of vocation for Moses, for me, for each one of us: "The One who sent me is with me, He has not deserted me, since I always do what pleases Him."

There could be no words so strong, yet at the same time so gentle: "I always do what pleases Him."

And this is only possible if I believe that He "is with me He has not deserted me."

CHAPTER V

" 'Get up and eat, else the journey will be too long for you!' " (1 Kings 19:7)

The God-who-is has always been searching for me. By His choice, His relationship with me is presence, as a call, as a guide; He is not satisfied with speaking to me, or showing things to me, or asking things of me. He does much more.

He is Life, and He knows His creature can do nothing without Him; He knows His child would die of hunger without bread.

But man's bread is God Himself, and God gives Himself to man as food.

Only eternal life can feed man who is destined for eternal life.

The bread of earth can nourish man only for this finite earth; it can sustain him only as far as the frontier of the Invisible. If man wants to penetrate this frontier, the bread from his fields is not sufficient; if he wants to march along the roads of the Invisible, he must feed on bread from heaven.

This bread from heaven is God Himself. He becomes food to man walking in the Invisible. The clearest indication of God's plan for man is the story of Elijah in the First Book of Kings. It is the most extraordinary adventure of a man searching passionately for God and allowing himself to be led along the mysterious paths of contemplation, beyond things, beyond himself, beyond history, beyond the frontier, with a food given by God Himself.

Just as Abraham is the founder of the race of believers, just as Moses is the symbol of anyone who marches from his own Exodus towards the Promised Land, in the same way Elijah is the prototype of whoever goes beyond earthly visions, beyond meditation and reasoning, beyond human conception of the things of God.

Let us think of him for a moment. Elijah is a committed man, committed totally. He is inspired by zeal for Yahweh. He has done all within his power—going far beyond mere duties—to establish the kind of "parish" which will conform with his dreams and his visions of good. He has killed Yahweh's enemies and put the priests of Baal to the sword; he has laid the spiritual foundations of a kingdom of power and glory, and he has established order in the country.

And he would have died happy, like some priest in a "Christian" country, where prostitutes are arrested by the police, and delinquent children put into schools by the Reverend Fathers.

But God has another vision of things. His plan is different, His sensibility finer. He is concerned not only with the police hauling off the wicked to justice; he is concerned with the wicked who are just as much His sons, and who are to be converted, not destroyed.

This revelation of a God of Love went quite beyond Elijah's powers of reasoning, as it went beyond the rest of the patriarchs.

It is easier for the wicked to conceive of a God who is strong, unconquerable, a castigator, a Lord of Hosts.

And here is God dragging Elijah beyond his own ideas.

At the same time he puts him into a state of crisis and makes him weak, because it is so difficult to explain things to someone who is always right, who always wins, who is absolutely sure of himself.

Elijah loses.

The powers are against him; he is even threatened with death.

So there he is at the limits of the wilderness, collapsed beneath a juniper tree, saying to his God: " 'This is enough, O Lord. I have had enough. Take my life, for I am no better than my fathers.' " (1 Kings 19:4).

A man in crisis begins to taste what he is too full of. Generally his wounded pride. "I am no better than my fathers." Elijah had really believed he was better than other men. He had done so much work for God. But with God he had mixed in himself, his own success, his own triumph.

How good to see the triumph of God lined up in procession behind Him! Just as it is pleasant to see our triumphalism camouflaged behind God's triumph!

But more than that.

53

A man in crisis begins to exaggerate; he starts running on a course opposite to the first.

If before he overestimated his own power, now he condemns it. If before he did too much, now, beaten, he won't do anything!

He closes himself in his isolation.

"Leave me, Lord."

But, instead, the Lord says: " 'Get up and eat, else the journey will be too long for you.' " (1 Kings 19:7).

This food given to Elijah on the edge of the desert may be seen as the symbol of a food which is to nourish man: The Blessed Sacrament.

And it will nourish him with eternal life and take him beyond the frontiers of this world.

The frontier is represented by the desert: "he walked forty days and forty nights to the mountain of God, Horeb." (1 Kings 19:8).

In biblical language forty signifies many, many. . . .

Patience is necessary to cross the desert; commitment is necessary for the purification the desert brings.

Above all, the desert means "to renounce."

Yes, renounce these stupidities upon which we have wanted to build our poor existence; renounce those ideas we have been clinging to; above all, renounce that attitude we have had towards heaven and towards earth: "I was right; you'll see I was right!"

In order to reach the contemplation of God's face, we must put aside the power of reason. Not just the desire of being right, but reasoning itself.

As long as we go on reasoning, we will not be ready for the vision of God.

That is why contemplation begins when we no longer meditate, we no longer question, but we *let ourselves be acted upon.* Every one of us must write this above an important chapter of his own existence, the chapter in which he enters the way of contemplation.

Let yourself be acted upon.

At last Elijah lets himself be acted upon, and, reaching Horeb after the purification of the desert, he is ready for God's revelation: "Go outside and stand on the mountain before the Lord, the Lord will be passing by."

A strong and heavy wind was rending the mountains and crushing rocks before the Lord—but the Lord was not in the wind. After the wind there was an earthquake—but the Lord was not in the earthquake. After the earthquake there was fire—but the Lord was not in the fire. After the fire there was a tiny whispering sound. When he heard this, Elijah hid his face in his cloak and went and stood at the entrance of the cave. Then a voice said to him, "Elijah, why are you here?" (1 Kings 19:11-13).

The nature of sacrament is supernatural; the nature of contemplation is passive.

Contemplation comes from beyond. When I contemplate, I do not look inside myself, I look ahead of me.

What do my ideas matter? I know them, and they die one after the other.

What engages me in contemplation is an idea that cannot die, and this comes from God.

That is why I believe in contemplation.

One ounce of transcendence is dearer to me than any amount of reasoning.

If reasoning is there at all, it comes beforehand.

All my life I have been reasoning! Now I am trying

to do without reasoning for a time, while I lay myself before God and let Him act upon me.

I prefer to do as Elijah and wait for His coming in the cave of Horeb.

Contemplation is passive; it is God's coming into us, into our consciousness. God lets us know Him *as He is*, not as He may appear to be from outside.

In contemplation I attain the fullness of my earthly life and I feed on eternal life, because eternal life is what I am destined for. All the rest can take care of itself, because it counts for little compared with eternal life. "Seek first his kingship over you, his way of holiness, and all these things will be given you besides." (Matt. 6:33).

No, Elijah will not reach fulfillment in the fire, nor in the earthquake, nor in the wind, but in silence. That God-filled silence, in which you feel your soul reduced to a fragile stalk. But it is a stalk able to be filled with God's dew and become an ear of wheat for His granary.

Yes, that's the way it is.

If you asked me how God has revealed Himself to me I should reply, "He reveals Himself as newness."

I am not newness, I am old age. Everything in me is old, boring, repetitive.

But when I search God's face I find newness.

God is eternally new.

God never repeats Himself.

When I pray I search for this newness of God. When I contemplate I hope for His newness.

And it is the only thing that never bores me.

That is why I understand that if I do not pray I am

up against the wall of my "old age"; if I do not contemplate I am without "prophecy," if I don't nurse at the breast of divine life, grace is lost to me.

And who am I without the newness of God?

Who am I without prophecy?

What use am I without grace?

CHAPTER VI

" 'Let me go, for it is daybreak.' " (Gen. 32:27)

The revelation of a God who is love and not violence, communication and not disaster, newness and not oldness, is merely the beginning of God's plan for man, not the end.

God does not want merely to make Himself known to His creature; He wants to give Himself.

The whole process of man's glorification on earth ends in a union of which marriage is only the image.

> *I will espouse you to me forever:*
> *I will espouse you in right and in justice,*
> *in love and in mercy;*
> *I will espouse you in fidelity*
> *and you shall know the Lord.*

(Hos. 2:21-22)

If you ask a mystic who has had a real experience of God which is the most beautiful book in the bible, he will not hesitate to say *The Song of Songs* because it represents most nearly the epic of love between God and man.

> *The Bride:*
> *Let him kiss me with the kisses of his*
>   *mouth!*
> *More delightful is his love than wine.*
>
> (Sg. of Sg. 1:1)

> *The Bridegroom:*
> *Ah, you are beautiful, my beloved,*
>   *Ah, you are beautiful*
> *Your eyes are doves*
>   *behind your veil.*

> *You have ravished my heart, my sister, my*
>   *bride*
>
> (Sg. of Sg. 4:1,9)

> *The Bride:*
> *I was sleeping, but my heart kept vigil;*
>
> (Sg. of Sg. 5:2)

St. John of the Cross, perhaps the greatest mystic we have known, was reluctant to construct his *Canticles* on the same design as the biblical book, and he sings thus:

> *The Bride:*
> *To fetch my love more near,*
> *Amongst these mountains and ravines I'll*
>   *stray*

59

Nor pluck flowers, nor for fear
Of prowling beasts delay,
But pass through forts and frontiers on my
  way.

Oh who my grief can mend!
Come, make the last surrender that I yearn
  for
And let there be an end
Of messengers you send
Who bring me other tidings than I burn for.

How can you thus continue
To live, my life, where your own life is
  not?
With all the arrows in you
And, like a target shot
By that which in your breast he has begot.

Why then did you so pierce
My heart, not heal it with your touch sub-
  lime?
Why, like a robber fierce
Desert me every time
And not enjoy the plunder of your crime?

Come, end my sufferings quite
Since no one else suffices for physician:
And let mine eyes have sight
Of you, who are their light,
Except for whom I scorn the gift of vision.
Reveal your presence clearly
And kill me with the beauty you discover,

For pains acquired so dearly
From love cannot recover
Save only through the presence of the lover.

The Bridegroom:
Turn, ringdove, and alight
The wounded stag above
The slope is now in sight
Fanned by the wind and freshness of your
      flight.

The Bride:
My love's the mountain range
The valleys each with solitary grove
The islands far and strange,
The streams with sounds that change,
The whistling of the love-sick winds that rove.

Before the dawn comes round
Here is the night, dead-hushed with all its
      glamours
The music without sound,
The solitude that clamours,
The supper that revives us and enamours.

The Bridegroom:
Now, as she long aspired,
Into the garden comes the bride, a guest:
And in its shade retired
Has leant her neck to rest
Against the gentle heart of the Desired.

Now flowers the marriage bed

61

With dens of lions fortified around it,
With tent of purple spread,
In peace securely founded,
And by a thousand shields of gold surmounted.

The Bride:
Rejoice my love with me
And in your beauty see us both reflected;
By mountain slope and lea,
Where purest rills run free,
We'll pass into the forest undetected:

Deep-cellared is the cavern
Of my love's heart, I drank of him alive
Now, stumbling from the tavern
No thoughts of mine survive,
And I have lost the flock I used to drive.

The breathing air so keen
The song of Philomel: the waving charm
Of groves in beauty seen.
The evening so serene,
With fire that can consume yet do no
   harm."

(Spiritual Canticle)

If this were not true, we could say that man's greatest folly was to dream of such an intimate, absorbing, final relationship with the Royal One, with the Absolute, with God.

But it is truth. It is not folly! It is fruit of the Creator's immeasurable mercy; it is the greatness of

His divine love for man; it is one of the proofs of how He glorifies man in His rapturous plan of salvation.

Certainly you will always find common-sense people who are scandalized by reading the *Song of Songs*; they even consider it too dangerous for young people to read, but . . . what's the use!

Wasn't there once a time when the bible itself was considered dangerous reading? From fear of indigestion one prudently died from starvation. But let's leave the past and come to the present; let's leave the errors and come to the truth.

God wants to give Himself to man. God calls His people His bride. He calls His people Israel, the name given to all believers in Yahweh, to the tribe that boasts of being Yahweh's bride!

What is the culmination of love? Is it not union? The gift of oneself? The reciprocal, exultant delight of the "Other"?

And has not the God of Love stamped the entire universe with His seal?

Is not love the most universal song of creation?

Must the experience humanity has constructed and lived here on this earth with a son, a friend, a brother, a mother, a bride end in the lonely frost of the tomb?

If the construction of things were up to you, and you had designed the plan of creation, would you have given death the last word? Would you not have planned in such a way that you could carry loving on beyond earthly things, on beyond death?

Is God less inventive than we are?

Is God less desirous of making everyone happy?

No, we rest assured. Love will continue after death. Indeed, it will be greater.

At the same time, it will be more purified. It will have had the opportunity to free itself from the heavy dross of egoism, fear, introversion, jealousy. But it will remain, it will remain. Because love is the aim of existence.

The end of our life is the kingdom of God; it is the final agape, the eternal marriage feast of the Lamb.

And who will be the bride if not Israel, humanity, each one of us?

The whole Bible is nothing more than the announcement, the proclamation of the eternal marriage between Israel and Yahweh. And it is and must be the boast of God's people.

Why doubt? Why be afraid?

Israel is the bride of Yahweh!

But let us take a look at Israel before it became a symbol of each of us, when it was still called Jacob and still lived on this side of the Promised Land.

Jacob was the son of Isaac; the great Abraham was his grandfather. Like his grandfather, Jacob had Yahweh's promise, in an extraordinary moment of his nomadic existence. He happened to spend the night in a certain place. Resting his head on a stone he went off to sleep, and he dreamed:

> ... a stairway rested on the ground, with its top reaching to the heavens; and God's messengers were going up and down on it. And the Lord was there standing beside him and saying, " 'I, the Lord, am the God of your forefather Abraham and the God of Isaac; the land on which you are lying I will give to you and your descendents.

These shall be as plentiful as the dust of the earth and through them you shall spread out east and west, and north and south. In you and your descendents all the tribes of the earth shall find blessing. Know that I am with you; I will keep and protect you wherever you go ...'" (Gen. 28:12-15).

For Jacob this promise at Bethel provided the strength for his journey, the stimulus for his vocation. It accompanied him beneath the tents of his existence, throughout the ups and downs of a nomad's life.

The substance of his faith in Yahweh became ever more purified, and prepared him for the night of "passage."

God no longer called him Jacob, but Israel. This was the first announcement from Yahweh of the mystical dimension in the plan of salvation. At that time it represented the end of mankind's eschatological vocation.

In Jacob's maturity, he became aware of something extraordinary that was about to happen. God was acting like a magnet.

In the course of the night Jacob arose, took his two wives, and the two maidservants and his eleven children, and crossed the ford of Jabbok ... he took them across the stream and had brought over all his possessions ... (Gen. 32:23).

Then he remained alone.

The most extraordinary thing in his existence was about to happen.

Some man wrestled with him until the break of dawn. When the man saw that he could not prevail over him, he struck Jacob's hip at its socket, so that the hip socket was wrenched as they wrestled. The man then said, "Let me go, for it is daybreak." But Jacob said, "I will not let you go until you bless me." "What is your name?" the man asked. He answered, "Jacob." Then the man said, "You shall no longer be spoken of as Jacob, but as Israel, because you have contended with divine and human beings and have prevailed." Jacob then asked him, "Do tell me your name, please." He answered, "Why should you want to know my name?" (Gen. 32:25-30)

Images are signs, just as sacraments are signs, just as everything is a sign.

Signs indicate, they veil and unveil, they give life, they nourish, they explain, they relate God's mysteries to man.

These signs are like letters of the alphabet conveying the unknowable language of God to the limited and experimental knowledge of man.

The image of forbidden fruit indicates the mystery of sin.

The taking of Adam's rib for the creation of Eve foretells the unbreakable union between man and wife. In the same way, the imagery of Jacob's struggle encodes the entire mystery of prayer as a combat of love between man and God, the creature wrestling with his Creator.

Man wants to pass, and God does not let him pass, although He wants him to pass.

Man wrestles with God, and God is happy to see man's shoulder pressing on His own heart.

Man asks God to say "yes," and God refrains from

saying it, just to hear the infinite repetition of the request, louder every time.

The struggle on the bridge of passage, and the dialectic of love between God and man, between Yahweh and Israel, is the ever maturing awareness of man's "yes," and God's eternal "yes."

God resists man, because man's desire is still superficial, immature, childish.

God lets man weep, because man still needs to weep.

He lets man wait, because man still needs to wait.

Union is not yet mature, desire still lacks clarity.

A great struggle is still necessary, and the night is night just for this.

Then daybreak will come, and everything will change.

But as long as we are on this earth we shall keep wrestling, like Jacob on the bridge, with the visible and the invisible, the earthly city and the heavenly city, the natural and the supernatural, the health of the body and the eternal salvation of the soul, the desire to live here below and the hope of going up above, the hunger for bread and the insatiable desire for heaven, the dream of enjoying the seasons of life and the knowledge of entering the one eternal season of the Kingdom.

But the battle is long and demanding.

And we may become limp, as did Jacob, if for no other reason than to remind us that the conquest of God is not in the race, but in the patience of death.

Only afterwards will it be possible to enter completely into the Kingdom, and we shall be mature enough to embrace God chastely and with Him to embrace all creation.

That is why the catechism, as old as our grandfathers, but full of truth, says, "God created us to know Him, to love Him and to serve Him in this world and to be happy with Him in Heaven."

"To be happy" is here synonymous with "to possess." It conceals all the mystery of the final union with God, a union still denied to Jacob in his violence. Jacob will remain with us on this side of the bridge until the attainment of the new heaven and the new earth, sung in the *Revelation* and proclaimed by the hope of all the people of God who pray.

CHAPTER VII

" 'I Know the Messiah is coming.' " (John 4:25)

God presents Himself to man little by little. The whole story of salvation is the story of the God who comes.

It is always He who comes, even if He has not yet come in His fullness. But there is indeed one unique moment in His coming; the others were only preparations and announcement.

The hour of His coming is the Incarnation.

The Incarnation brings the world His presence. It is a presence so complete that it overshadows every presence before it.

God is made man in Christ. God makes Himself present to man with such a special presence, such an obvious presence, as to overthrow all the complicated calculations made about Him in the past.

"The invisible, intangible God has made Himself visible and tangible in Christ."

If Jesus is truly God, everything is clear; if I cannot believe this, everything darkens again.

The bible itself becomes obscure, and man awaits tearfully against the wailing wall for fulfillment of a prophecy which does not exist, or rather for one with no date, no place, no time, no space, no native land.

Believing in the Incarnation, believing that God was made man and lived among us, believing that Jesus was the son of God, means above all believing in the bible.

It is the bible which has spoken of Him and announced His birth (cf. Isa. 7:14). It indicated the place where He would be born (cf. Mich. 5:1-3). It specified His origin and genealogy (cf. 1:7,11). It foretold His behavior among men (cf. Isa. 8:23; 9:1, 49; 58:6, 61:1-2), His character (cf. Isa. 42), His tastes, His poverty, the way He would be treated and betrayed (cf. Isa. 50:52; 13:53).

And the bible, eight centuries before His coming, outlined His sorrow-filled portrait. The brush was Isaiah's, and we might even call him the fifth evangelist.

He grew up like a sapling before him,
like a shoot from the parched earth;
There was in him no stately bearing to
make us look at him,
nor appearance that would attract us to him.
He was spurned and avoided by men,
a man of suffering, accustomed to infirmity,
One of those from whom men hide their faces,
spurned, and we held him in no esteem.
Yet it was our infirmities that he bore,
our sufferings that he endured,
While we thought of him as stricken,

> as one smitten by God and afflicted.
> But he was pierced for our offenses,
>   crushed for our sins;
> Upon him was the chastisement that makes us
>   whole,
>   by his stripes we were healed.
> We had all gone astray like sheep,
>   each following his own way;
> But the Lord laid upon him
>   the guilt of us all.
>
> Though he was harshly treated, he submitted
>   and opened not his mouth;
> Like a lamb led to the slaughter
>   or a sheep before the shearers,
>   he was silent and opened not his mouth.
>   Oppressed and condemned, he was taken away,
>   and who would have thought any more of his
>   destiny?
> When he was cut off from the land of the living,
>   and smitten for the sin of his people,
> A grave was assigned him among the wicked
>   and a burial place with evildoers
> Though he had done no wrong
>   nor spoken any falsehood.
> But the Lord was pleased
>   to crush him in infirmity.

(Isa. 53:2-10)

Who is this colossus striding across the whole story of salvation, who is present at every stage of the march of God's people? He is the awaited One, he is Emmanuel, he is God with us, he is the Anointed One of the

Lord, he is the Messiah, he is He who is to come, he is God's Christ.

Try to take His presence out of the bible if you can.

It is difficult to believe in Jesus of Nazareth, it is much more difficult not to believe.

I cannot free myself from Him, even if I want to.

His presence has entered into me so completely that denying it for me would mean denying light.

I can, certainly, but by sinning against the Spirit.

And then, to whom shall we go for light? Does a prophet greater than the Nazarene exist on the horizon of my life, or your life?

Does one exist?

Does a man exist who has said and done greater things than He did?

Try to think.

Put together everything that has been said about God and men. Make the comparison with the "religious men" from all the earth of all time, and tell me if there is one to equal Jesus!

No, such a one does not exist, cannot exist.

Not for nothing does Jesus seal a prophecy, and time itself begin again with His coming.

Even the years of history begin to count again from zero, and our souls find a new birth standing before Him.

> "I solemnly assure you,
> no one can see the reign of God
> unless he is begotten from above."

(John 3:3)

Beginning again, being born again, for us means

making easy the way, marching more quickly, ˢ
ing everything.

St. Paul understood it in a flash and got furiouˢ ᵃt
those who wanted to hold on to the past after Jesus,
wasting time mixing up circumcision with Baptism.

Christ has freed us from the past with its infinite
complexities. In Him we have become "new creatures"
and begun a new life, owing nothing to anyone, writing
in our book, "Now I am beginning . . ."

What matter is your past, your sin? Now walk in the
newness you have found and sin no more.

But it is not enough.

To facilitate the march in the "newness of life" Jesus
destroys casuistry and puts Himself in the place of all
the laws and books of morals in just one sentence:

"You heard the commandment imposed on your
forefather . . . What I say to you . . ." (Matt. 5:21,
22).

He becomes the living Book, the custom, the tradi-
tion, the Law, the Only One.

What I just did was to give you an example:/as I
have done, so you must do. (John 13:15)

This is my commandment:/love one another/as I
have loved you. (John 15:12)

Jesus seals the past, closes the period of waiting, and
becomes incarnate in history.

After His coming there is no more need to search; it
is enough to fix our eyes on His person.

Imitation of His life becomes the norm. Believing in
Him becomes not only salvation but *eternal life.* " 'He
who believes has eternal life.' " (John 6:47).

A new humanism is born with Him, from the earth
and the heavens, from the visible and invisible, from

human hopes and divine hopes, from the earthly city and the heavenly city, from the son of man and Son of God.

Indeed, with Him, every man may become a son of the Most High, glorified flesh, an impregnable creature, a divine tent, a holy one of God, an inheritor of the Kingdom.

Yes, the Word was made flesh, God was made man.
Man has seen God on earth.
John says something that touches us deeply at the distance of centuries. In unparalleled words he writes with rousing witness:

> This is what we proclaim to you:
> what was from the beginning,
> what we have heard,
> what we have seen with our eyes,
> what we have looked upon
> and our hands have touched—
> we speak of the word of life.
>
> (1 John 1:1)

How existential is this beautiful sentence of John's: "What . . . our hands have touched."

Yes, Jesus, God on earth, was touched by men, handled, gazed on.

Men saw Him weep, eat, sleep, speak, walk, suffer, use a whip. They saw Him go out alone into the night to pray; they saw Him on the lake, reproving and appeasing the wind and the sea; they saw Him heal the sick, bring Lazarus to life; they heard Him speak of the Kingdom, standing before the temple of Jerusalem.

How many memories were engraved in the minds of His friends, those whom He called on to follow Him. Memories which came back alive and stirring even after His departure.

"We who were with Him on the holy mountain," Peter wrote as he walked the consular roads of the Roman Empire.

And Peter remembered what had taken place on Mount Tabor, on a day so filled with light. In that memory and that face so extraordinarily transfigured into the divine, he found strength to reach the end of his demanding witness—to walk to martyrdom, without turning back, when he still could have done so.

If Jesus is God-made-man it is certain that there must be a radical change in man's history. If God's Absolute has entered history, no further history exists.

With the Incarnation humanity became the "divine family" and man became God's blood-relation through Christ.

If it is true—and it is—that God became one of us in Jesus, it is not something of small importance: man's hopes now have an extraordinarily solid basis.

Jesus, who is God, is my brother, so my heart need no longer be filled with fear.

The horizon of our whole existence has changed with a brother such as God.

What interest can I have in my ancestor's vineyard since the hour that I entered God's vineyard with my brother, Christ? What does my father's inheritance matter to me, since the hour I became an inheritor of Christ Himself?

The proportions have changed with my entrance into a Kingdom that has no proportions.

Listen to how Paul becomes exultant before the vision of the new reality that man has begun to take part in with the Incarnation of Jesus:

> Praised be the God and Father of our Lord Jesus Christ, who has bestowed on us in Christ every spiritual blessing in the heavens! God chose us in him before the world began, to be holy and blameless in his sight, to be full of love; he likewise predestined us through Christ Jesus to be his adopted sons—such was his will and pleasure—that all might praise the glorious favor he has bestowed on us in his beloved. (Eph. 1:3-6)
>
> Listen to how he summarizes the plan of salvation: God has given us the wisdom to understand fully the mystery, the plan he was pleased to decree in Christ, to be carried out in the fullness of time: namely to bring all things in the heavens and on earth into one under Christ's headship.
>
> In him we were chosen; for in the decree of God, who administers everything according to his will and counsel, we were predestined to praise his glory by being the first to hope in Christ. (Eph. 1:9-12)

That is not bad for poor creatures like ourselves!

It seems a dream to speak of these things to men who are pulling in their belts from hunger, or crying from morning to night, tormented by numberless wounds, sitting on the dungheaps of the world, like Job on his.

And yet this, and only this, is the substance of faith and the mainspring of hope; it is great only because it is obscure and sorrowful.

We are God's heirs!

We are saints, even if we are still sunk in sin. We are risen in Christ even while we suffer in our limbs the poison of our deaths.

Even if our eyes are dimmed by sorrow and our hearts are frozen by the terror of things we cannot understand and by the fringe of a crowd crying out "Crucify Him!", with the invincibility of a faith that does not fail, we fix Christ in the middle of the battle and say with Paul:

> He is the image of the Invisible God, the first-born of all creatures. In him everything in heaven and on earth was created, things visible and invisible, whether thrones or dominations, principalities or powers; all were created through him, and for him. He is before all else that is. In him everything continues in being. It is he who is head of the body, the church; he who is the beginning, the first-born of the dead, so that primacy may be his in everything. It pleased God to make absolute fullness reside in him, and, by means of him, to reconcile everything in his person, both on earth and in the heavens, making peace through the blood of the cross. (Col. 1:15-20)

CHAPTER VIII

" 'Our Father who art in heaven . . .' " (Matt. 6:9)

The incarnation of the word of God, the coming among us of Jesus, the presence of Christ in history, is the incarnation, the coming, the presence of the Witness to the Absolute, the only One who is able to speak to us in the language of heaven. Indeed, He says Himself: " 'No one has gone up to heaven / except the One who came down from there— / the son of Man who is in heaven' " (John 3:13).

Clearly, if nobody has been there, nobody can tell us what is up there.

Only Jesus can be a witness to heaven, to the invisible, because only He comes from there. His mission among us is first of all to give witness.

He knows, He has seen, He has heard.

He can tell us: " 'I tell you what I have seen in the Father's presence' " (John 8:38).

He can affirm with strength:

" 'But I know Him/Were I to say, 'I do not know Him'/I should be no better than you—a liar' " (John 8:55).

To whom does Jesus give witness? Of whom does He speak? With whose presence does He fill the invisible heavens?

He gives witness to the Father's existence; He speaks of Yahweh and calls Him Father; He fills the kingdom of God with the presence of the Absolute, first defined by Him as " 'my Father and your Father . . . my God and your God' " (John 20:17).

The mission of Jesus begins right here: revealing the Father's existence to us, speaking about Him to us, giving witness to Him.

Immediately, with no reticence, He speaks of His dependence on Him:

> —*"The Truth is*
> *I have not come of myself*
> *I was sent by One who has the right to send*
> *There is one who sent me and I really come from*
> *   Him"*

(John 7:28)

> *"For I have not spoken on my own;*
> *no, the Father who sent me*
> *has commanded me*
> *what to say and what to speak'*

(John 12:49)

He states His unconditional obedience:

". . . I always do what pleases Him"

(John 8:29)

". . . the Son can do nothing by himself."

(John 5:19)

He speaks of the Father's love for Him:

"For the Father loves the Son
and everything the Father does He shows him.
Yes, to your great wonderment,
he will show him even greater works than these."

(John 5:20)

He tells of His complete love for the Father:

"Doing the will of him who sent me
and bringing his work to completion
is my food."

(John 4:34)

From the dawn to the sunset of His earthly life, the presence of the Father was the "divine environment" of Jesus. From His baptism in the Jordan, when, as He came up out of the water, "he saw the sky rent in two and the Spirit descending on him like a dove. Then a voice came from the heavens: 'You are my beloved Son. On you my favour rests.'" (Mark 1:10), until His death on Calvary, "'Father, into your hands I commit my spirit.'" (Luke 23:46), the presence of the Father was Jesus' point of reference for His interior life, for His contemplation, for His discourse. How many nights did He go out under the stars just to be alone with the Father; how many times words of union with Him came to His lips: "Father, it is true. You have graciously willed it so" (Matt. 11:26). He exulted in the Father's actions: " 'Father, Lord of heaven and earth, to you I offer praise; for what you have hidden from the learned and the clever you have revealed to the merest children.' " (Matt. 11:25); he confirmed his vocation to give revelation and witness for the Father: "Everything has been given over to me by my Father. No one knows the Son but the Father, and no one knows the Father but the Son—and anyone to whom the Son wishes to reveal him" (Matt. 11:27)

So, if we accept Jesus as Son of God, we must also accept the Father as a quite distinct presence. The gospels are quite incomprehensible if we exclude the dialogue, the relationship between Jesus and His Father. It is a symbol, a model of each dialogue and relationship between us and God.

The solemn prayer Jesus used during the Last Supper to sum up His earthly mission is so clear that it leaves no doubt He is speaking with the Absolute God:

After he had spoken these words, Jesus looked up to heaven and said:

> "Father, the hour has come!
> Give glory to your Son
> that your Son may give glory to you,
> inasmuch as you have given him authority over all mankind,
> that he may bestow eternal life on those you gave him.
> (Eternal life is this:
> to know you, the only true God,

81

and him whom you have sent, Jesus Christ.)
I have given you glory on earth
by finishing the work you gave me to do.
Do you now, Father, give me glory at your side,
a glory I had with you before the world began."

(John 17:1-5)

Yes, Jesus reveals the Father and gives witness to Him. He is the One who knows everything about Him.

He speaks about Him as though He saw Him, as though He were in continuous communion with Him, as someone with whom He has always lived and whose character, tastes, habits, and way of life He knows.

This is what is so marvelous about the gospels—nothing could have replaced Jesus in this mission. Through His words we come to know God Himself, His exact will, His way of looking at things, His most intimate desires, His holy countenance.

But what is even more marvelous—in fact, divine—is that throughout the accounts of the precise words and the detailed experiences of Jesus, the mystery of God's face remains total, the night of divine Transcendence is as thick as it was in the temple of the first covenant. We are obliged to live on faith, hope and love, just as we always were.

Jesus does not shift the balance in the relationship between creature and Creator. This balance rests only on man's act of abandonment and God's act of gratuitous love.

I should say that, although Jesus has given us the "photograph" of the Father in the gospels, the mystery, the "unknowing" of God remains. We see, and yet we do not see; we become acquainted, and yet we still need to become further acquainted; we know, but we are still very ignorant. It is a photograph that we are able and unable to see.

It depends on you. You are the camera, able to fix inside yourself what you see and what you don't see in the gospels and thus to make a photograph of your own. You know that the power of fixing an image in the soul depends on the Holy Spirit, who is love, who alone is able to make that photograph in proportion to your intimacy with Him.

For example, after a careful reading of the gospels, ask yourself if you succeed in understanding anything definite about hell.

"God is so good," you exclaim. "God is love, God is a Father, God is merciful . . ."

And above these comforting words you hear the Scripture shout out: "Beware of falling into the hands of the living God!" It is the same Jesus speaking, who a minute ago had been describing the love of the Father through the parable of the prodigal son, with everything finishing in a feast. Now He tells a rather different parable, one about Dives, with the banqueter ending in Hell!

Try to reconcile these two gospel texts if you can:

"Love your enemy and do good; lend without expecting repayment. Then your recompense will be great. You will be called sons of the Most High, since he himself is good to the ungrateful and the wicked" (Luke 6:35).

"Then he will say . . . 'Out of my sight, you condemned, into that everlasting fire prepared for the devil and his angels' " (Matt. 25:41).

No, you can't reconcile them.

No, you can't, and that is why it is dangerous and childish to form over-simplified ideas about God's thoughts and to express rash judgments about Him.

After twenty centuries of meditating on the gospels, at every turning point in history, man has been faced with new situations and found himself unprepared, as though before an enigma.

In his hands, the gospels seem like a closed book which has to be completely rediscovered and, still more, freed from the fetters of past cultures and ideologies in which preceding Christians have bound it.

Then one begins wondering about the most essential, common things: the supernatural versus politics—verticalism versus horizontalism—immanence versus transcendence—human revolution versus eschatological revolution.

And if one does not take care, one can set out unwittingly on quite a wrong road—live with the renouncing angelists in a hypothetical, spiritualist heaven; or turn to the error of reincarnating Jesus' message in a new culture or ideology which is destined, like all the others, to perish, incapable of expressing God's thought and fit only to be a vehicle of suffering for Christians yet to come.

No, it is not easy, even for the Church, to read in the message of Jesus that even though we are His intimate spouse, we can become distracted by the things of earth, and we constantly run the risk of either saying old things which serve no purpose or being silent when we should speak.

In the gospel of Jesus, God remains a mystery. The face of the Father, which Jesus came to trace out for us here on earth, remains the face of the unknowable One. Let us not forget it.

But there is a way to unveil the unknowable, to read His intimate thoughts, to gain knowledge of Him—the way of love.

That way is to enter the enclosure of love, guided by love, so that we can reach knowledge of the Father: "He who loves, has eternal life." And eternal life is knowledge of God.

Indeed, Jesus began in such a way, speaking to us of love, making us enter His enclosure, training us for the difficult task of knowing how to love. And he always set His Father in the place of the One who knows how to love.

And He knows how to love in a way that is quite different from the way in which we sinners almost always love:

> To you who hear me, I say: Love your enemies, do good to those who hate you; bless those who curse you and pray for those who maltreat you. When someone slaps you on one cheek, turn and give him the other; when someone takes your coat, let him have your shirt as well. Give to all who beg from you. When a man takes what is yours, do not demand it back. Do to others what you would have them do to you. If you love those who love you, what credit is that to you? Even sinners love those who love them. If you do good to those who do good to you, how can you claim any credit? Sinners do as much. If you lend to those from whom you expect repayment, what

85

merit is there in it for you? Even sinners lend to sinners, expecting to be repaid in full. (Luke 6:27-34)

Not bad!

It's difficult to find a text which expresses more clearly the striking, drastic contrast between our way of loving—full of self-interest—and God's true way of loving—unselfish.

This way of loving unselfishly, gratuitously, Jesus attributes to the Father.

This is what He says: " 'Love your enemy and do good! Lend without expecting repayment. Then your recompense will be great. You will rightly be called sons of the Most High, since he himself is good to the ungrateful and the wicked' " (Luke 6:35).

Then He reinforces this idea by adding: " 'Be compassionate, as your Father is compassionate' " (Luke 6:36).

But how is the Father compassionate?

How can I find the answer in what Jesus gives witness to in the gospels?

I read the parable of the prodigal son, and I find it easy to agree, now that my daughter has run away from home and I am ready for anything—just so long as she returns!

I read the parable of the man who could forgive a friend a debt of ten thousand talents ($10,000) . . .

This is more difficult to forgive—at least for a good administrator, for someone used to being thrifty. Nevertheless, if my debtor has no more money, if I get mixed up with lawyers I'll have to pay out still more . . . so I'll make the best of it and forgive him.

But where I begin to have difficulty in understanding is further on, where it is a question of the poor and the innocent, where, by letting things go, I compromise other people.

Is the Father merciful to torturers?

Is He merciful to those who cling to power by letting the poor go hungry? To those who let a baby die of starvation in the midst of their millions? To those who sell armaments and consciously stir up quarrels, falsify the news, spread dissent, and see war only as an opportunity to make more sales?

Is He merciful to dictators who transform power into a terrible weapon, capable of debasing all life, of suffocating God's gift of freedom in prisons?

Is He merciful to racists, who separate men from each other according to the color of their skin, committing horrible, violent crimes to turn themselves into gods?

What does Jesus answer me?

Nothing, that I know of. He is silent.

He Knows that if things remain the way they are, the Father will apply the condemnation in defense of the poor, recorded by Matthew: " 'Out of my sight, you condemned, into that everlasting fire. . . . I was hungry and you gave me no food' " (Matt. 25:41-42). There's no joking with the poor! The Father must take up their defense.

But why is Jesus silent?

Why doesn't His gospel offer exhaustive replies to the problems troubling mankind? Why doesn't Jesus, who knows the Father, tell us how to deal with them?

Love gets complicated sometimes!

How can you go on loving a torturer, a capitalist who starves people, a proud racist, a gun merchant?

Yet, love is invincible and it is for all mankind. This poor man who sins in such an outrageous way can still be saved, he can find some escape.

And if the love is the love of God Himself, will the God-who-is-man not find it?

Here is how He will find it.

In the silence he will experience what it is like being the victim of every act of violence, every calumny, from all the powers of this world.

He will experience what it is like to be imprisoned, tortured, mocked, sold, condemned.

And when he has experienced all this, knowing the degree of the Father's love, and how tragic is the condemnation which man risks, He will hand down His opinion on justice, invoked from the cross of His suffering, from the very stones of Calvary. In that moment the whole of history will ask him how to act, and He will give the most extraordinary reply of love. He will cry out an excuse for man's sickness of mind: " 'Father, forgive them! They do not know what they are doing' " (Luke 23:34).

In that moment, I, too, hope that the love of the Father will save me from my many evil deeds, and from my frightening insensitivity towards the poor of the whole world, because I knew not what I was doing.

CHAPTER IX

". . . and He saw the Spirit of God descending like a dove . . ." (Matt. 3:16)

There is a third Presence in heaven and on earth. In addition to Jesus and the Father, there is a third Person seeking us,

It is the Holy Spirit.

Jesus Himself told us about Him, giving witness to His life:

" 'This much have I told you while I was still with you;/ the Paraclete, the Holy Spirit/ whom the Father will send in my name,/ will instruct you in everything,/ and remind you of all that I have told you' " (John 14, 25:26).

When He speaks of the Spirit, Jesus seems to want to announce a time of fullness, a time which is more extraordinary, a time which is more complete for man:

" 'I have much more to tell you,/ but you cannot bear it now./ When he comes, however, being the spirit of truth/ He will guide you to all truth . . .' " (John 16; 12-13).

We could say that without this third Person, there would be no progress, that the truth revealed by Jesus could not reach its fullness, that we could not even understand what He said, that, well, there's something missing—yes, missing.

Moreover, this third Person who is to come, whom the Father will send in the name of Jesus, never acts alone nor speaks on His own:

" 'He will not speak on his own,/ but will speak only what he hears,/ and will announce to you the things to come' " (John 16:13).

That is strange to anyone who does not understand, but it is not strange to anyone who understands that Jesus never seeks a personal autonomy, but always refers to others, to a kind of council.

First, during the years that He lived with His own, He always referred to the Father:

" 'For I have not spoken on my own;/ no, the Father who sent me/ has commanded me/ what to say and how to speak./ Since I know that his commandment means eternal life,/ whatever I say/ is spoken just as he instructed me' " (John 12:49-50). Then, at the end of His earthly life, in the intimacy of His last hours living among men, when He was already heading towards the beyond, He refers to the Spirit.

Speaking of Him, He testifies clearly and without reticence, that this Person, the Spirit, " 'will not be speaking on his own . . .' " (John 16, 13).

This is an evident reference to the convergence of the divine Persons, which theologians call the Trinity, and to what the unexpected overflowing of the Spirit reveals from within it.

Indeed, the Trinity is the intimate life of God.

Indeed, the Trinity is love, and only love can reveal to us.

Jesus had good reason to say " 'I have much more to tell you,/ but you cannot bear it now' " (John 16:12).

How is it possible for us to understand God's intimate life without specific personal revelation from Him to us?

At this point, we, like the apostles, are truly at the rise of a new dawn. Jesus' revelation about the Trinity is the beginning of the final renewal of the world.

Success in grasping at the mystery of the Trinity means being able to enter the same divine home, the family bosom of the Absolute, the very life of God. And success is possible only through love.

Only God's love for me can open the doorway of His intimate life. And the Holy Spirit is the love which opens that door and allows me to contemplate the intimate life of God.

Only the love He diffuses in me, through the grace given by Christ, can enable me to see the "things of above."

The Holy Spirit is communication: communication between the Father and the Son, and communication between us and God.

If He is there, everything is clear; if He is not, everything is dark.

Do not ask me to understand on a human level. I can't.

It is enough for me to contemplate, and it is the

91

Spirit who gives me the power to contemplate: He is the love of God in me.

The catechism is not enough, theology is not enough, formulas are not enough to explain the Unity and Trinity of God.

We need loving communication, we need the presence of the Spirit.

That is why I do not believe in theologians who do not pray, who are not in humble communication of love with God.

Neither do I believe in the existence of any human power to pass on authentic knowledge of God.

Only God can speak about Himself, and only the Holy Spirit, who is love, can communicate this knowledge to us.

When there is a crisis in the Church, it is always here: a crisis of contemplation.

The Church wants to feel able to explain about her spouse even when she has lost sight of Him; even when, although she has not been divorced, she no longer knows His embrace, because curiosity has gotten the better of her and she has gone searching for other people and other things.

The revelation of a triune God in the unity of a single nature, the revelation of a divine Holy Spirit present in us, is not on the human level; it does not belong to the realm of reason. It is a personal communication which God alone can give, and the task of giving it belongs to the Holy Spirit, who is the same love which unites the Father and the Son.

The Holy Spirit is the fullness and the joy of God.

It is so difficult to speak of these things. We have to babble like children, but at least, like children, we can say over and over again, tirelessly, "Spirit of God, reveal yourself to me, your child."

And we can avoid pretending that knowledge of God could be the fruit of our gray matter.

Then, and only then, shall we be capable of prayer; borne to the frontier of our radical incapacity, which love has made the beatitude of poverty, we shall be able to invoke God's coming to us, "Come, creator Spirit!"

God is not a solitary.

That is why He is not alone.

He is a Trinity.

If He were only unity, He would be a solitary. But, being love, He is a Trinity, Father, Son, and Spirit.

The Father is life, and He is the source of all things; the Son is the image of the Father, and He is light; the Holy Spirit is the love which unites them, and He is a divine person.

God, being love, is communication.

The scene in which man most easily pinpoints this mystery on a human level is baptism of Jesus, as reported by the evangelists.

"Jesus . . . came directly out of the water. Suddenly the sky opened and he saw the Spirit of God descend like a dove and hover over Him. With that a voice from the heaven said, 'This is my beloved Son. My favour rests on Him' " (Matt. 3:16-17).

That's it: there is the Father, there is Jesus, and there is this third divine person, the Spirit.

And, as in the famous scene where Jesus identifies Himself with the lamb because of its meekness and vocation to sacrifice, so here the Spirit is identified with the dove because of its mobility and its gentleness.

The Holy Spirit is Love.

He is God communicating Himself to us and speaking to us of His intimate life.

He says to us: We are three, and We are One alone.

Before this revelation we could consider Jesus alone or speak to the Father alone.

We can't any longer.

With the coming of the Spirit, who is the fullness of the revelation, we can no longer catch hold of one of the Divine Persons without the other two being present.

With the coming of the Spirit, we shall always be led back, carried towards the unity of God.

Love is never alone; now that we have the revelation of love, we cannot look at ourselves alone, we cannot look at God alone.

Look at Jesus on Calvary: see the dove of the Holy Spirit on His head, and, above, the face of the Father, near His beloved.

It is always like that.

Wherever Jesus is, there we shall find the Father.

Wherever the Father is, there we shall see Jesus.

Where the Father and Jesus are, there we shall see the Holy Spirit.

No longer are we able to pray to one of the divine persons without feeling the presence of the other two.

It is a continuous dialogue which drags us into the bottomless whirlpool of unity, through the undying fire of triune love.

Indeed, the triune love of God is called "charity," and it is something quite different from ordinary human love, and far greater.

The one is as far from the other as the heavens are

from the earth. Indeed, this is the distance between the way in which we love as creatures, and the way in which Christ loves.

That is why it is simply discouraging to hear Christians speaking of love as non-believers do, making a human message out of the gospel.

And it is still more discouraging to reduce Christian prophecy to programs for social advancement and the development of peoples. Without doubt, these programs are of basic importance, but they are certainly not summaries of Christianity.

Love is preached by practically all religious faiths, even by secular creeds.

Examples of love can be discovered in an atheist.

But that love is not the love Christ brought to earth, the love by which all will know us as His disciples (cf. John: 13:35).

This other love, the love of Jesus, is a love which is profoundly theological, the love called charity, the love for man and for the world which was lived by Christ during His earthly existence and is lived now in a mediate way by those who adhere to Him in faith and hope.

The triune love of God which lodges in the hearts of those who believe in Jesus is the badge of the Christian: it characterizes his actions; it is the life of all his other loves; it is the authentic divine life in man.

The Holy Spirit, whom the Father sent us in the name of Jesus, carries the fullness of divine life to the center of our being. This is not only the presence of God within us, but the dynamic way in which God loves. It is this unmistakable "costume" of God's which Jesus revealed to us by living on this earth: " 'I give you a new commandment:/ Love one another, such as my love has been for you,/ so must your love be for each other.' " (John: 13:34); " '... love one another/ " (John 15:12).

Jesus did not love like a human creature; He loved as God loves.

That is an enormous difference!

The way Jesus loved was the life of the Trinity within Him.

The love of the Trinity is the new kind of love proposed to man. But it is impossible to live it without the Trinity within us.

That is why the Christian is "inhabited."

He is "inhabited" by the Trinity.

" 'Anyone who loves me/ will be true to my word,/ and my Father will love him;/ we will come to him/ and make our dwelling place with him' " (John 14:23).

PART II

In the fullness of time God places Himself in the reality of man. With the coming of the Holy Spirit at Pentecost man becomes God's dwelling place. From now on man lives out the covenant with God through the dynamics of history; within his earthly limits, man waits for the last coming of the One who has no limits.

CHAPTER X

"We will come to him and make our dwelling place with him." (John 14:23)

I am a dwelling place.

I am not alone.

In the secret depths of my poor human substance is the presence of God.

Not a God who is a solitary, but a God who is Trinity, a God who is love.

A God who is Father, a God who is a Son, a God who is Holy Spirit. But a God made One by love.

And a God whose love enables me to become one with Him: " 'that all may be one/ as you, Father, are in me, and I in you;/ I pray that they may be one in us/ that the world may believe that you sent me,' " (John 17:21).

I believe that no moment exists for man which is more important, more beautiful, more dramatic, more decisive, more radical, than the moment when he becomes aware of—or rather, "lives"—this reality.

When God reveals Himself in His nature as one and in His actions as three, Pentecost penetrates the depths of man's heart.

His soul is enflamed and He becomes inebriated with light and with life.

It is as though he were going beyond his own limits, leaving his old earthly city, to enter the new land of God.

For the first time he touches the frontier of Christianity, he is aware of the nature of the Kingdom.

The first thought that comes to his mind is the superior value of this new discovery; he really adopts the attitude of the man who decided to sell everything to buy "that field" (cf. Matt. 13:44) or to acquire "that one really valuable pearl" (cf. Matt. 13:46).

Then his way becomes full of a new security, a security he has never felt before, a security that is complete and joyful and dynamic, a security that destroys fear just as food destroys hunger. It gives meaning to the words of Jesus: " 'Do not live in fear, little flock. It has pleased your Father to give you the Kingdom' " (Luke 12:32).

Security and plenitude!

For the first time man experiences what it means to need nothing more. God alone is sufficient—just as Jesus said: " 'On that day you will have no questions to ask me' " (John 16:23).

Yes, you do not have to ask when God is at the center of your being, when you contemplate His way of loving, when, in His infinite goodness, He makes you enter into this "way of loving."

What can you ask for when you possess everything?

And there is more.

At the same moment in which you discover—or rather, live—the experience of the Unity and Trinity of God within you, you discover and live the unity of your human existence.

You need no longer ask yourself, "Who am I?"

You know it, see it, you live it.

By finding God in you, you have found yourself.

Now you know who you are! You have no more questions to ask.

For there are not many mysteries, there is only one. Having discovered that one, a God who is Trinity and Unity, you have discovered the rest. Rather, you have seen Them.

Now you can agree with what Jesus says, " 'You will have no questions to ask. . . .' "

This is fullness lived on this earth, contemplating the Unity and the Trinity of God, the way in which God loves Himself and loves us in Himself.

What comes from this is peace. A peace which is complete and divine, a peace which makes even this exile on earth sweet. A peace which was promised us by Jesus: " 'I give you my peace,' " a peace that brings the comfort that is necessary to us who still live so far and yet so close to Him, even within Him.

The enigma is right there: God has already come, and yet He is coming and He will come, as the kingdom which is already within us while we march towards Him.

It is the movement of the Trinity, which is a movement of love, which is inexhaustible.

You love, and you will love yet more.

You are within, and you must enter yet further within.

And this movement will never end, not even in Heaven, because the love of God will grow within you infinitely.

That is exactly how it is.

God has already come and is still to come. God is in me, and I, like the bride, am still waiting for Him in the darkness of faith, in the tension of hope, in the gift of charity.

Anyone who is unaccustomed to God's dynamic may find this strange, but nothing is truer than that this is the way God acts.

He came out of light into creation, He will come yet more in Adam.

He came in Jacob, but He will come yet more in Elijah.

He came in Abraham, but He will come yet more in Paul.

The God who comes proceeds with time, with history; He places himself in the geography of the cosmos.

This is why everything is holy, and why you can feel His presence in all matter, but you can feel it infinitely more in the bread of the Eucharist.

Everything is advancing towards man's being taken up into God, towards his transformation into a son of God.

There is a presence in the seed, there is a presence in development, there is a presence in the fullness of being.

God is in the seed. God is in the development. God is in the fullness.

102

That is why He came, is always coming, and will come. The waiting is ours.

Praying means waiting for Him to come; living means accepting that He has come; dying means hoping that He will come.

Up to the end.

And when He comes for the last time in history, it will be our Apocalypse, the moment of absolute maturity, of marriage, of banquet, of eternal possession.

The new heaven and the new earth ring like the Messianic proclamation of a time when the fullness and the exultation of possession by God will replace the old heaven and earth which God did not yet possess because of our resistance to Him, but which He was already searching for.

CHAPTER XI

"I opened to my lover—but my lover had departed, gone." (Sg. of Sg. 5:6)

To have found God, to have experienced Him in the intimacy of our being, to have lived even for one hour in the fire of His Trinity and the bliss of His Unity clearly makes us say: "Now I understand. You alone are enough for me."

Then the most beautiful phrases of the Song of Songs come true, and we live repeating to God the words of love invented for man's most intimate relationships on this earth:

> *The Bride:*
> *Let him kiss me with kisses of his mouth!*
> *More delightful is your love than wine!*
> *Your name spoken is a spreading per-*
> *fume—*
> *that is why the maidens love you.*
> *Draw me!—*

(Sg. of Sg. 1:2-4).

The Bride:
Tell me, you whom my heart loves,
*   where you pasture your flock,*
*   where you give them rest at midday,*
Lest I be found wandering
*   after the flocks of your companions.*

(Sg. of Sg. 1:7)

The Bride:
Hark! My lover—here he comes
*   springing across the mountains,*
*   leaping across the hills.*
My lover is like a gazelle
*   or a young stag.*
Here he stands behind our wall,
*   gazing through the windows,*
*   peering through the lattices.*

(Sg. of Sg. 2:8-9)

Then we come to understand the dimensions of heaven; then we see things as they really are, and we see God as really God!

But then, too, we realize that this cannot last, that in order to keep its gratuitous quality, the fragrance of that hour must be paid for in a harsh and severe way.

Perhaps because it would all be too beautiful?

Perhaps because contemplation would destroy the roots of action?

Perhaps because you would never again get anything done, as though you were on too perfect a honeymoon?

Perhaps because heaven would start here and now, whereas the way is still long, and possession of the Beloved is feeble?

Yes, all this and many other things are true.

But there is one other thing which seems to me still more true, and I understood it only very late:

You would not be free any longer.

And God is terribly concerned about your freedom in loving Him.

He knows that you can be suffocated by the greatness and the quantity of His gifts.

It is difficult to make a marriage between two persons who are in such different circumstances.

He brings you His all, while you can only bring Him your nothing.

How can one set about reconciling such differences?

How can He be certain that you are not seeking Him out of self-interest?

That you are not going to Him only because you have found no one else?

That you are not going to Him for the pleasure you get out of it?

That would be too easy and too shallow a love.

When the bible says that God is a jealous God, it is speaking truly.

But God's jealousy is not like ours.

He is jealous because He is afraid that, instead of loving Him in His naked being, we love His creation, His riches, His gifts, the joy He bestows, the peace He brings, the truth He makes us a present of.

God is not only jealous in His love. He is tragic.

Before making you His, before letting Himself be possessed, He tears you to shreds—rather, He makes history tear you to shreds.

Here is what He does:

The Bride:
I was sleeping, but my heart kept vigil;
    I heard my lover knocking:
"Open to me, my sister, my beloved,
    my dove, my perfect one!
For my head is wet with dew,
    my locks with the moisture of the
        night."
I have taken off my robe,
    am I then to put it on?
I have bathed my feet,
    am I then to soil them?

My lover put his hand through the opening;
    my heart trembled within me,
    and I grew faint when he spoke.
I rose to open to my lover,
    with my hands dripping myrrh:
With my fingers dripping choice myrrh
    upon the fittings of the lock.
I opened to my lover—
    but my lover had departed, gone.

(Sg. of Sg. 5:2-6)

That is what He does. Just when you have decided to
be His, He escapes . . . far off.
    Indeed:

The Bride:
    I sought him but I did not find him;
        I called to him but he did not answer
            me.

107

The watchmen came upon me
as they made their rounds of the city;
They struck me, and wounded me,
and took my mantle from me,
the guardians of the walls.
I adjure you, daughters of Jerusalem,
if you find my lover—
What shall you tell him?—
that I am faint with love.

(Sg. of Sg. 5:6-8)

For much of my life, I asked myself why God acted in such a strange way.

Why is He silent so long?

Why is faith so bitter?

He can do everything, so why does He not reveal Himself to men in a more sensational way?

What would it cost Him to come out into the streets, among the men who cry "God does not exist," give a hard slap to the noisiest, and say—better still, shout—"Don't believe these fools! I am here indeed! To convince you, let's make an appointment to meet tomorrow evening in Leningrad's museum of atheism. You'll see what I'll do! I'll crush you and reduce you to souvenir envelopes!"

But it seems that God does His best to remain silent, as if to demonstrate that He does not exist, that it is useless for us to follow Him, that we would do better if we went all out to possess the earth.

And are there not men who, when faced with His silence, convince themselves that He does not exist? And are there not others who are scandalized merely by the way the world goes?

108

If God exists, why evil?

If God is love, why sorrow?

If God is a Father, why death?

If I have knocked, why has He not opened to me?

I used to think all this and more, when I was new to this school.

But then, walking patiently, not allowing myself to become frightened off by the first difficulties, hounding His door with the determination of a man on a hunger strike, and, above all, believing His gospel true and unrelenting, I began to see the way things are, I began to discover how God goes about what He is doing, I began to distinguish His stealthy footsteps.

I was no longer amazed that He treated me like the the bride of the Song of Songs, that He escaped when I opened the door.

It was for Him to open it, not me, always in a hurry.

Sin lies in Adam's haste, and my lust for possession is stronger than my true love for Him.

Wait! Oh, the anguish of that "wait," the emptiness of that absence!

But then, little by little, I began to understand, as never before, that He was present in the emptiness, in the waiting.

I was thirsty for presence, so, in order to stretch out my desire, He presented Himself as absence. Therefore, I was obliged to purify my faith and tell Him I believed in Him, not out of self-interest, but out of love.

I was thirsty for His light and truth, so He presented Himself as darkness.

Until that moment, I had never understood the

meaning of the cloud which guided the people of God in the desert.

If you want God's embrace, if you want to reach the Promised Land, you must accept the scandal of all the things you don't understand right to the limits.

There is always something irrational about love; there is always something of what we call folly in this synthesis of mysteries.

Was not Jesus clothed in folly before being clothed in blood?

But it is not enough.

I wanted possession of Him, so He presented Himself as insensibility in the cold desert dawns.

"Before accepting your embrace I want proof of your fidelity.

"You are too sensual for Me to give Myself as food for your desires which are so poor in love, and so saturated with egoism.

"You believe you love Me, but in reality you are loving yourself.

"It is always the same!

"You must make some progress before leaving yourself and what is yours!

"For your sake I left what was mine and came to you.

"You do the same.

"Wait for me all your life as though I were coming every evening. I shall be present, and you will not see me; I shall be your lamp, and you will not realize it; I shall embrace you, and you will not feel anything.

"Then I shall know truly whether you love God because He is God, or whether you love Him because He is the solution to your problems."

A God always runs this risk.

"I want to protect Myself.

"You must love Me because I am Love, not because I am pleasing to you."

Yes, love, not power. Love, not tranquility. Love, not pleasure.

That was when I understood what was meant by naked faith, hope without memory, charity without pleasure.

I understood that God does not reply to our wild raving because He is purifying us with sorrow and with death.

He wants to accustom me to His jealousy.

He wants to make me to accept profoundly the concept that for Him sin is synonymous with betrayal, and not with omissions of the law, weakness, possible mistakes, bad taste or immaturity.

I say to you as emphatically as possible: do not try to corrupt God. You will not succeed—not even as well as does a woman who tries to bribe her lover by seducing him.

God is as inexorable as death in His love for us. He is ready to wait until the Last Judgment, but He will not change His ideas about our selfishness. So, let me tell you, you need patience!

Do not expect to have the Beatific Vision after ten minutes of recollection.

Do not seek for pleasure or enjoyment in prayer and do not wrap yourself round with clouds of sentiment.

Do not go out hunting for God as the latest curiosity in your life or as the last lover in your old age.

Accept faith as it is—naked. Wait all your life for the God who is always coming, and who does not show

Himself to satisfy your curiosity, but unveils Himself before your faithfulness and your humility.

Accept the hope that is the indelible trace which He has left in the depths of your soul, an infinite nostalgia for heaven. Accept charity as God's way of loving, which meant abandoning His beloved Son to the torments of Calvary for the salvation of all the world.

Perhaps the abandoned Jesus is the model for the greatest test of love, our strongest support in those moments when we feel really alone?

A story which could be true comes to mind.

A young engaged couple. Wonderful. Beauty, health, identical points of view, and, more important, identical conceptions of the gift of oneself.

They wait for the day when they will become one and proclaim with the risen Christ their union as a sacramental sign of victory and dominion over oneself.

A road accident: the car overturns on a curve. The flaming petrol attacks the young girl's body.

When her fiancé succeeds in dragging her out from the twisted wreckage, her physical beauty is ruined forever and she will be burdened by permanent infirmities.

"Will you still marry me?"

"Yes, I shall marry you, because in you I have loved something that goes beyond your body."

Well, this man and woman will be able to understand why God wraps Himself in naked faith to make Himself loved by us.

CHAPTER XII

"God chose those whom the world considers absurd to shame the wise; he singled out the weak of this world to shame the strong." (1 Cor. 27)

In asserting that God presents Himself to us as absence, darkness, silence, I run the risk of being told, "You're exaggerating!"

Yet I have experienced that that is the way it is.

And going from experience to the bible it has been easy to find texts to bear it out. What a help it has been, this profound discovery of how God reveals Himself to us. It has really turned my way of thinking upside down.

Let us now look together at its main pattern. Each of us can go into the details for himself afterwards.

Well, mankind is waiting for God. The Chosen People, which are like the vanguard on the march and consequently more aware of waiting, fix their eyes on the horizon. By now the Messiah must be near.

What are these people, His People, looking for in Him?

What characteristics do they expect when they see Him for the first time?

Power, glory, blinding light, triumph.

What happens?

Weakness, smallness, obscurity, anonymity.

Who cared about God's coming, veiled in the flesh of a defenseless child?

No one!

Mary, the poor mother of Jesus, clasps in her arms the "Unknown One" of the people, the true "Hidden God" of Isaiah.

Those who were waiting were blind.

Nobody moved from Jerusalem, the holy city, the footstool of the throne of God!

No, worse! Someone did move, but only in order to murder this nuisance who had not come in the way He was expected.

The most religious people on earth, the Chosen People, were living only on that waiting, and it had become spasmodic, it could be felt in the air.

What were they searching the horizon for, at the advent of the Messiah, at the dawn of all the prophecies?

The son of David, the conqueror, the God of Hosts, He who was to restore the Kingdom, He who would finally oppress the hated Romans! Triumph, victory, safety . . . always the same!

What happened?

A poor workman, hidden in an unknown village—and the most despised one at that.

No good. After so many years, no one realized what had happened.

Their eyes were searching for something quite different than the sweat of a laborer or the anonymity of a poor man!

And how does the story end?

The clash between Him who says He is the Son of God, the Messiah, and those who cannot accept such goings-on reaches a climax; it closes with the crucifixion of an innocent man.

Bethlehem, Nazareth, Calvary are demonstrations of God's silence and God's poverty, real roads that he traveled in order to come to us and make Himself known.

And they are darkness.

Oh, not darkness for Him, or in themselves, for nothing is more luminous than the annihilation of Jesus at Bethlehem, the reality of the incarnation at Nazareth, the infinite love streaming from Calvary.

That is light, and what light!

But for us, who want noise, God is silence; the light is darkness.

Darkness for us who want power, while God is meekness.

Darkness for us who want pleasure, always pleasure, while God is service and gratitude and love, often painful love.

Even the Church, which should be intimate with God's thoughts, makes continual blunders in this sense and on this road.

She knows well enough that He said: " 'My kingdom does not belong to this world' " (John 18:36); yet she makes herself a kingdom, the Vatican, tiny though it may be.

She knows well enough that the tenderness and nonviolence of Jesus prompted Him to tell Peter, " 'Put your sword back in its sheath' " (John 18:11); yet since, slyly and deceitfully, she has put quite a few to death through "zeal" for Him.

She remembers, how she remembers, that He came to Jerusalem on an ass, never accepted being made king, and always escaped from triumph; yet she, poor little thing, has often settled comfortably into the earthly kingdom and loved triumph—so much so that the word "triumphalist" was coined just for her.

It is difficult to believe in God, difficult to understand His intimate thoughts, and still more difficult to listen to Him. And it is quite easy to claim rightfully the title "Bride of the Lord," and yet we find ourselves carried into ways that certainly displease Him because they are contradictory to His thoughts.

Yet we must not even be scandalized. We must face the reality of human weakness. It is infinite, but it does not surpass the mercy of God.

Now I am no longer amazed when I see darkness between Him and me, when between His thoughts and mine there is shadow, incapacity to understand, when He replies to my thirst for His embrace by absenting Himself and leaving me in the bitterness of a prolonged wait.

I know that it is all a question of my faith, which is the first serious trial of my love for Him.

Faith is like the placenta surrounding the foetus; that foetus is myself, still incapable of looking at the light.

Faith is like the period of betrothal, in which I am

116

still able to say "no" to Him, if I don't see clearly the path I am to follow.

Faith is like the protection He offers my freedom in love.

But faith is also the power I have in my life of showing Him the love which has been freely given to me.

Faith is the possibility of walking towards Him, not urged on by self-interest or the usual thirst for the enjoyment of possessions, but only by the desire to please Him.

Faith is the true proof of love.

Faith is my true wealth, my only strength.

If God is great and comes to me with the immensity of creation, I go to Him with the grandeur of being accepted as a creature.

If God is love and comes to me with the folly of His cross, I go to Him with the folly of my faith.

If God is freedom and comes to me accepting the risk of my freedom, I go to Him accepting the risk of my faith.

My faith is never greater than when I live it out in the darkness which often acts as a shadow for my sick eyes.

I am not saying that it is easy to grasp God's thought all at once—anything but! I am only saying that faith gives me power to believe in what I do not understand.

And that is why faith is not always apparently rational.

I do not blame Jesus' contemporaries for not understanding Him, but I am amazed that they did not believe.

The greatness of Abraham did not lie in his having understood, but in his having believed. He had sufficient signs for belief; he was logical in his faith, rather than his reasoning.

How could the patriarchs understand the plan of salvation when it was still enclosed in the heart and mystery of God?

They simply believed, and in this they gave us a good example, as St. Paul says in his letter to the Hebrews:

"All of these died in faith. They did not obtain what had been promised but saw and saluted it from afar. By acknowledging themselves to be strangers and foreigners on earth, they showed that they were seeking a homeland" (Heb. 11:13-14).

This all means something very important for us, something that can overturn our way of thinking about our relationship to God, that can give quite another meaning to the days of our earthly existence.

Man is something absolute, radically autonomous and free, and God does not unleash his autonomy and freedom.

In each of us the primitive chaos lives on; as Genesis says ". . . darkness covered the abyss" (Gen. 1:2).

But upon each one of us, as then, "God's Spirit hovered over the water" (Gen. 1:2).

In each one of us Adam is speaking with God, fleeing from God, sinning, and, unfortunately, being able to conceive Cain in a lustful embrace, which is to make him weep for his whole life.

But in each one of us the mercy of God carries faith as it did to Abraham, gives a vocation as it did to

118

Moses, implants a thirst for prayer as it did to Elijah, gives hope as it did to Jacob.

All these giants of the past are in us—rather, we can live the same dramas as they did, the same divine realities—and we are marching with them towards the coming of Christ.

Then, with the mystery of the incarnation, Jesus comes to us, as He did to Mary, and we can live out divine intimacy in all its fullness.

The whole bible is lived out in us, is spoken in us, and is mingled with our blood, with our experience, with our love.

Everything turns into hope in a God who comes, but who makes us experience the suffering and the waiting of advent, the lament of Jeremiah, the peace of Amos, the images of Hosea, and the visions of Zechariah.

But for this to become alive, my "yes" is necessary, my free and loving acceptance.

Often such an acceptance is easy, obvious—reasonable, we should say.

But it is often dark, and sometimes painful.

Then my love becomes involved, and faith becomes proof of it.

In that moment chattering counts for nothing, as Jesus Himself warned me: " 'None of those who cry out 'Lord, Lord' will enter the kingdom of God' " (Matt. 7:21).

It is facts which count—plain facts.

Take a simple example.

When her husband is near and does not let her want for anything she expects, hopes for and enjoys, a wife says she loves her husband, says it easily and normally. But when the husband is far away, when the waiting is prolonged for months and years, when doubt grows that he will ever return, oh, then the true test of love begins!

What light, what splendors in the possibilities this wife has to resist, while she fixes her eyes on the anonymous crowd and tries to pick out him, only him!

What power of real, living, strong testimony emanates from the faithful vigilance, the unquenchable hope, which this woman lives behind the bitter doorway of waiting!

Oh, how each one of us would like to be the bridegroom who returns disguised as a poor stranger, whom she does not recognize, but to whom she repeats, again and again, her certainty of his return and the sweetness of his love!

Well, every evening, when the darkness wraps itself round my prayer, He, God, is there, disguised as a poor man watching me.

When I endure, in the darkness of faith, the prolonged wait for the God who comes, He has already come to me and is embracing me silently, with the same embrace with which I, in faith, embrace Him.

CHAPTER XIII

"The Messiah—that is Christ—is coming."
(John 4:25)

It sounds like a fairy story, yet it is the truth. God became bread in Christ. God comes to me hidden in a piece of bread!

In the last chapter we finished by saying that the bridegroom would come disguised as a poor stranger to find the bride waiting for Him, and that all of us would desire to be approached in such obscurity by the object of our love.

Well, the Eucharist is such poverty of God, it is such a hiding place of God made near to us, it is such a coming of God into the intimacy of our dwelling in pure faith. If you think about it, it stuns the mind. Either Christ is a raving madman, or He is truly omnipotent and merciful Love, who has found the most direct road to our hearts, a road that will not frighten or scare us, a road that is as simple as could be.

Consider Christ's presence under this sign of bread.

121

From the beginning of this book we have been talking of a presence, the presence of a personal God.

God made Himself present in Adam as creation, became voice in Moses, conscience in Abraham, experience in Elijah, intimacy in Jacob.

As though that were not enough, He became Jesus, visible and tangible presence; Father, in His most profound revelation; Holy Spirit, in the fullness of the gift of Himself.

It might have been enough. Men in search of God do not lack appointments and meeting places; they only have to want to find Him.

But, the inventiveness of God, the creativity of God, found another way of making His presence concrete, of realizing His presence among us, near us, before us, close to us, within us.

He became transformed into a piece of bread.

> ... the Lord Jesus on the night in which he was betrayed took bread, and after he had given thanks, broke it and said, "This is my body, which is for you. Do this in remembrance of me." In the same way, after the supper, he took the cup, saying, "This cup is the new covenant in my blood. Do this, whenever you drink it, in remembrance of me." (1 Cor. 11:23-25)

It is difficult to believe Christ's words, which are so tremendous and amazing.

But it is equally difficult to get away from them.

I can not avoid them any longer, and if I did, I should be sinning against the Spirit.

That is why I say, "I believe in what Jesus said; I believe that this bread of life is Christ near me, Christ become bread for me, and Christ become presence in me."

I know that this act of faith is dark as the night, but nothing is clearer than this night.

I have gazed for days and days at this bread, I have lived for weeks in caves in the desert with this presence alone, and always, always He has said to me in faith, "It is I, do not be afraid. It is I, and I love you.

"Do not be afraid of the darkness, be a child before my words.

"I wanted to become bread to be eaten by men, because by eating Me, they are feeding upon eternal life.

"Why do you find it strange that I should have wanted to become bread through love?

"Have you had no experience of love?

"When you have loved, really loved, have you not wanted to become bread for your beloved?

"Oh, to be able to enter the body of the person you love!

"Would not a mother do this for her child?

"Does not the bridegroom do this for the bride?"

You can argue about the Eucharist as much as you like, but on the day love really takes hold of you, perhaps you will understand that Jesus is not a fool or a madman.

To be able to become bread!

To be able to nourish the whole world with His flesh and blood!

I am terribly selfish and fearful when faced with suffering, but if I could become bread to save all humanity, I would do it.

If I could become bread to feed all the poor, I should throw myself into the fire at once.

No, the Eucharist is not something strange: It is the most logical thing in the world, it is the story of the greatest love ever lived in this world, by a man called Jesus.

When I gaze on this bread, when I take up this bread into my hands, I gaze on and take up the passion and death of Christ for humanity. This bread is the memorial of His death for us. This bread is the trumpet call of the Resurrection, through which we, too, shall one day be able to rise.

This bread is the living summary of all God's love for man.

From Genesis to the prophets, from Exodus to the Apocalypse, everything is yearning towards this terrible mystery of God's tragic love for man. God, who made Himself present in the first covenant and yet more present in the Incarnation, becomes still more present in this mystery of the bread of life.

You can hold God in your hand as a piece of bread; it is a close, personal presence.

Only His glorious presence in the Messianic banquet will be greater than this actual presence of His in a piece of bread, which I shut up in my traveler's pack as I walk the roads of the kingdom.

You can carry It with you.

Oh, how I hope that the time will soon come when after Mass every Christian will carry the Eucharist home with him!

When every Christian will construct a tiny oratory to honor the presence of God in the intimacy of his home, so he can gain from this mystery the strength to love and the joy to live.

In the mystery of the Eucharist, in the sacrament of the bread of life, God truly becomes everything to everybody.

Everyone can see Him, touch Him, take Him, eat Him, contemplate Him, locate Him, and finally, if he wishes, spend as much time with Him as love urges him to.

All this without agitation, without false fears, without the dangerous pressures of our senses, without the sloppiness caused by sentimentality.

If He were before us in another way—more striking, more pleasurable, more triumphal—we should be oppressed by it, or at least afraid.

So, under the sign of bread He leaves us completely free; He acts only on our faith, of which it is the great mystery; He stimulates our hope, of which He is the "memorial"; He revives our charity, of which He is the nourishment and the model.

Truly, the Eucharistic presence is an extraordinary thing! Only God could find such so clever, so close a way of being present without bringing in dangerous complications for the sensitivity, the pride, the sensuality, the selfishness of man.

We know all too well what happens to immature servants and young clerks when the master or the boss is around.

They become insincere so easily; they become agitated trying to show their zeal; they flatter in order to get on in their career; often they prostitute themselves in order to please those who are stronger.

We must not forget that we ourselves are immature servants and young clerks.

But there is nothing of all this with God. He leaves us in the office all our lives without ever showing Himself. He leaves us in the field behind the plough, telling us He has left and will return at the end of time.

And yet He is there, right there, and faith and love reveal Him to you as you go about your work, near you in the field, hidden in a piece of bread you carry in your sack.

He is watching you.

And he says nothing, nothing at all.

That way He is able to tell the true degree of your love. Rather, just because He is not the boss or the inspector, He leaves you at His disposition all the time so that you may mature in true love for Him and learn from Him.

And love Him with gratuitous love.

And love Him because He is light, not because He is pleasing to you.

And love Him because He is life, not because He is a secure haven of comfort.

But without meaning to I have gone a step ahead of myself. In the first place He is there as food.

Bread is food.

The Eucharist is food.

Before being friendship, God is bread. Before being your judge He is your food. In fact He has said: " 'I did not come to condemn the world but to save it' " (John 12:47).

He is not the boss watching me, He is the brother who feeds me.

And He is the food which transforms me.

He would have set out on a useless journey if He had come to prove my misery, my weakness, my ease in debasing myself.

Much better to come to change me.

He changes me by giving Himself in nourishment.

He changes me by letting Himself be consumed by me.

Read the entire discourse of Jesus in the synagogue of Capernaum, as John reports it.

This scandalous discourse, incomprehensible to an outsider, this crisis-sounding enigma for most people, from then onwards shines with His linear simplicity, obscure only for our powers of reasoning:

> *"Let me solemnly assure you,*
> *if you do not eat the flesh of the Son of*
>   *Man*
> *and drink his blood,*
> *you have no life in you.*
> *He who feeds on my flesh*
> *and drinks my blood*
> *has eternal life,*
> *and I will raise him up on the last day.*
> *For my flesh is real food*
> *and my blood real drink.*
> *The man who feeds on my flesh*
> *and drinks my blood*
> *remains in me, and I in him.*
> *Just as the Father who has life sent me*
> *and I have life because of the Father,*
> *so the man who feeds on me*
> *will have life because of me.*

*This is the bread that came down from
  heaven.
Unlike your ancestors who ate and died
  nonetheless,
the man who feeds on this bread shall live
  forever."*

(John: 6:53-58)

What can you understand of this discourse if you do
not accept it with the soul of a child, believing deep
down that the God who is love really wanted to give
Himself as food for all of us?

And in Him, desire and being are the same thing.

So, He came to us.

And He comes every day.

And He feeds us with eternal life.

And eternal life is He Himself.

We feed upon God.

And that is why, little by little, we become co-heirs
with Christ.

Sons of the Father.

People of God.

As we raise up the chalice of the new covenant, we
announce the Messianic era, when, at the table of love,
we shall feed on love and breathe love, which will make
us one with love: God Unity and Trinity.

CHAPTER XIV

> " 'Eternal life is this: to know you, the only true God, and him whom you have sent, Jesus Christ.' " (John 17:3)

God became bread in Christ to nourish us with eternal life. " 'He who feeds on my flesh and drinks my blood has eternal life.' " (John 6:54).

But what is this eternal life Jesus is speaking of? He has defined it Himself: " 'Eternal life is this: to know you, the only true God, and him whom you have sent, Jesus Christ.' " (John 17:3)

We cannot blame Jesus for any lack of clarity: "Eternal life is knowledge of God."

It is true authentic knowledge.

That is why I call the God of my faith the "God who is," not the "God who seems to me to be."

Anyone who feeds with truth on the Eucharist, anyone who believes, can say with strength, "I know my God, and I am basing myself on the very words of

Jesus: " 'He who believes has eternal life.' " (John 6:47).

I believe, therefore I have eternal life, therefore I know Him.

Indeed, how could God give me the commandment of love—("You shall love the Lord, your God, with all your heart, and with all your soul, and with all your strength") (Deut. 6; 5; Matt. 22:37; Mark 12:30; Luke 10:27)—without at the same time giving me knowledge of Him?

How can I love anything which I do not know?

Don't tell me that you don't know God, you who believe in Him and communicate with Him in the Eucharist!

If that were true, it would mean that you were communicating with the corpse of an idol; with a mummified commandment of the law, not with the living God.

But don't you know that God is alive? And that only the living can communicate with each other?

God communicates with me, and by communicating He gives me knowledge of Himself, just as by communicating with Him I can tell Him about myself.

I tell Him about myself, and He tells me about Himself. And the Eucharist, taken in faith, is the vehicle.

But it is not very important for me to tell Him about myself, for me to make myself known to Him, because He has always gone before me and does not need me to speak in order to know me. He already knows everything about me.

*O Lord, you have probed me and you know
me;
you know when I sit and when I stand;*

you understand my thoughts from afar.
My journeys and my rest you scrutinize,
with all my ways you are familiar.
Even before a word is on my tongue,
behold, O Lord, you know the whole of
it.
Behind me and before, you hem me in
and rest your hand upon me.
Where can I go from your spirit?
from your presence where can I flee?
If I go up to the heavens, you are there;
If I sink to the nether world, you are
present there.
If I take the wings of the dawn,
if I settle at the farthest limits of the sea,
Even there your hand would guide me,
and your right hand hold me fast.

(Ps. 139:1-10)

It is much more important for Him to tell me about Himself, for Him to speak to me of that kingdom from which He comes and to which I must go, following Him who is the Way. This is very important!

Coming to this earth, Christ brought us the knowledge of God. Becoming food for each one of us, Christ carries into us the revelation of the things of Heaven.

Feeding upon Christ, I enter the "Invisible," I enter Heaven, I begin an immense process of development within myself, I receive the knowledge of God which must lead me to the maturity of "sonship."

The Eucharist brings me knowledge of God: feeding upon Christ as food of eternal life makes me become

131

co-heir with Him, like Him, as intimate with the Father as He is.

Naturally for this to happen fully, we must reply to the Eucharist. This reply is prayer, which is the dynamics of living faith.

He comes to us, but we must go to him; He comes to us in food, but we must make a gift of ourselves.

The Eucharist is dead without prayer, just as faith is dead without works.

You cannot make love by yourself.

Love by yourself remains sterile and empty: it has no reply to welcome and to fertilize it.

We cannot listen to God's "yes" without offering Him our "yes."

God's "yes" is the sacrament of the Eucharist; our "yes" is prayer.

Here, I think, is the real reason for the frequent unfruitfulness and sterility of the sacraments; they are just performed as rites, to which one can no longer reply with living, personal prayer.

The Eucharist given to a man who does not pray is like food given to a corpse: it increases the smell.

Prayer, which is a reply to the "yes" of God's love, fertilizes the Eucharist in us and transforms It into life.

It is too easy to receive Communion; it is much more difficult to remain motionless for a quarter of an hour, thinking of what has been done, forcing ourselves in dark faith to bind our wills to the will of Him who came to find us with such gratuitous love.

It is a mistake to hide from this knowledge for too long or to make the excuse that the Eucharist will act on its own.

The Eucharist acts, gives life, fertilizes, only if we are alive, and being alive means believing, loving, praying.

Let us return to the example of conjugal love.

The fruitfulness and life of the marriage cannot be left to just one of the partners for too long. Either they must love together and really seek one another, or sooner or later there will be a crisis and then divorce (even "Italian style," which they dare not declare in the open).

Prayer is faith in action, the well-spring of hope, the conversation of love. There is no substitute when we truly want to possess eternal life, when we really become conscious of God.

Anyone who does not pray cannot know God's intimate life (which in theology is called charity). He can only know Him from the outside, as a symbol, as an idea, as a philosophy, as a science, as a number, as space, as eternity.

It is not enough to study theology or advanced exegesis to know God.

God's intimate life is unknowable to man.

He is "veiled" to man.

He only makes Himself knowable, He only unveils Himself, when we come before Him in an attitude of love, not in an attitude of curiosity.

Prayer, true prayer, is precisely the attitude in which man must present himself before God in order to enter His intimate life, which is the life of the Trinity.

> "that all may be one
> as you, Father, are in me, and I in you;
> I pray that they may be one in us,

133

*that the world may believe that you sent
  me.
I have given them the glory you gave me
that they may be one, as we are one—
I living in them, you living in me—
that their unity may be complete.
So shall the world know that you sent me
and that you loved them as you loved me."*

(John 17:21-22)

I must repeat once again—I cannot say it too
often—the relationship of man-God, God-man is sym-
bolized in marriage.

Marital love is an image, however pale, of the reality
which develops little by little between the Absolute and
the creature, between God and man, between Yahweh
and Israel.

In marital love it is not enough to study the beloved,
write poems, or receive cards from far away. Couples
must marry, say "yes" to one another, go behind the veil
of intimacy, delight in one another—exultantly, become
close, cultivate friendship, stay together as much as
possible, coalesce their wills, make two things one, as
scripture says.

But pretending to know the other just by studying
him in books or photographs means remaining outside
real knowledge, real mystery.

Today, many persons who seek or study God do just
that. They study Him in books, make Him an object of
speculation, approach Him from intellectual curiosity.

With what result? The more we study, the more our
ideas become confused; the more we get caught up in
discussions, the farther we go from Him.

I think this is the nature of the crisis in the Church today: it is a crisis of prayer, it is a crisis of contemplation.

Study is no longer the light of spirituality, and curiosity has taken the place of humility.

Self-assurance and derision of the past are the false light which guides man's pride in the labyrinth of God's "unknowing," pretending to seize the truth with the strength of intelligence only.

But God's truth is the same, truth is the secret of things "up there," and no one can know it without revelation from God.

Has Christ not already said so?

In the upper room, replying to the worried question put to Him by Judas (not Judas Iscariot) about why He was not manifesting Himself to the world, but only to His intimate friends, He replied with extreme clarity: " 'Anyone who loves me will be true to my word, and my Father will love him; we will come to him and make our dwelling place with him' " (John 14:23).

Only love brings God's coming to us, His living presence within us, and His consequent revelation.

> *"He who obeys the commandments he has*
>   *from me*
> *is the man who loves me;*
> *and he who loves me will be loved by my*
>   *Father.*
> *I too will love him*
> *and reveal myself to him."*

(John 14:21)

" 'I will reveal Myself to him.' " Here is all the

secret of contemplative prayer, all the hope man is searching for, all the faith for anyone who wants a living contact with God.

That is why I go to pray, that is why I get up in the night and place myself in the Presence of God, that is why I wait for the God Who comes, just as Israel waits for Yahweh, just as the bride of the Song of Songs waits for the Bridegroom.

I know God reveals Himself to anyone who loves Him, who searches Him out, who does His will; that is why I wait in prayer for His revelation.

I know that His revelation is personal, intimate, adjusted to whoever is standing before Him in faith; that is why I strive for personal prayer, why I am not content with a generic relationship with God.

I know that His revelation is concerned with the things "up there," the kingdom of the invisible, the intimate life of Yahweh; that is why I am not satisfied with considering the gospel message as a social message nor a psychological message, nor the stimulus for human revolution, however, radical and total.

It is Heaven I am seeking, not just earth, which is the tent I must leave one day.

It is the unknowable I am seeking in divine life, not the knowledge which is already in me and is terribly tiresome because I have already measured it and gone beyond it.

It is the life of the Trinity I am seeking so as to pass beyond my own limits, not earthly love which sucks at my heart and leaves me in my selfishness.

That is why I pray.

I pray because I am searching, and I know there is One who knows how to be found.

And I have no need to search far because the love He has for me has thrust Him very near.

When He is near He speaks and tells me about His own things.

His own things are eternal, infinite. His own things have no need of understanding, things such as the Trinity. It is enough to contemplate them.

And contemplation makes you see beyond everything.

Beyond yourself.

Beyond your limits.

Beyond your poverty.

Beyond your sin.

Beyond human history.

Beyond death.

CHAPTER XV

Jesus said to Peter, " 'Put your sword back in its sheath.' " (John 18:11)

One of the most fundamental errors a Christian can make in our times is to mistake or identify the gospel message with the evolution of history or with social revolution. It is an error of our age, and therefore easy to make.

Why?

The man of today—Christian or Buddhist, atheist or believer, Chinese or American—is discovering new depths in man and the scientific and technical possibilities of organizing himself a bit better in this world.

The discoveries of Marx and Freud—just to cite the best known—although in many ways incomplete and exaggerated have obliged mankind to face the problems hiding under the ashes and have encouraged men to find some solution.

Progress is inevitable; the military torturers of some

developing countries, the colonialists, the racists, the totalitarian governments cannot stop it. Anything but!

It is useless to oppose the history of certain ideas; sooner or later they will triumph.

Mankind is making an enormous leap towards equality, the just distribution of wealth, a sense of freedom and of brotherhood among peoples.

The power of the mass media has become such that facts cannot be hidden any longer—which was once easy to do—so the problems, the uneasiness, the suffering, the injustice of a small people or even of a single defenseless man are shared by millions, who are determined to band together in order to wipe out that injustice, that uneasiness, that suffering.

But these millions of men who suffer before their television sets and wring their hands about the injustices of the world are not all Christians.

Faced with the facts of suffering, of torture, of exploitation, of people being chained by ignorance and hunger, all men explode with the same energy, be they Christians or Communists, black or white, Muslims or Buddhists.

I can not say, I can not testify that I have seen Christians explode with greater energy than others; no, I just can not. Just as I can not say that Christians as such are better technicians, better doctors, better union leaders, better politicians than non-Christians.

Within the Marxist revolution I have seen the suffering man defended with the energy of a saint. In Africa I have heard young Muslims and Socialists with the courage of martyrs defend the right of little people to exist.

Everywhere there are men and women of every faith

139

willing to go to prison to accelerate the development of peoples. On the social horizon of the exploited there are not only the papal encyclicals, even the most modern ones of Pope John and Pope Paul.

No, the development of peoples, technology, astrophysics, medicine, culture, art, politics, are not confided more to the gospel than to any other text.

They are not more the theme of Jesus than of Engels or of Einstein.

This needs explanation.

God gave man the task of setting the earth in order—to cultivate and care for it—(Gen. 2:15).

The social message, the stimulus for all revolutions, is not in the gospels, but in Genesis.

Adam is the all-time revolutionary, not Jesus.

And all men are in Adam; all men are not yet in Jesus.

God did not wait until the coming of Christ to send His message of equality and justice to the people. He sent it at the creation of man; He gave it at the same moment in which He breathed the Spirit upon him.

Man as created by God is already capable of understanding that one must not live on the blood of the poor, and that white skin is not more precious than black.

Jesus drives home the concepts expressed by the Father at creation; He insists on them with greater strength, but His message goes further.

He did not come to free us from the chains of capitalism; He came to free us from the more painful, more radical chains that make every one of us at heart a capitalist—sin and death.

He did not come so much to speak of earth, which

we knew more or less already, as to speak to us of what is beyond this earth, of the nature of our existence and of His mystery, of the meaning of our vocation and of its importance.

He came to speak to us about the Invisible because we already had the visible under our noses and, after such a long history, we should have ordered it better.

And this visible world, this material to be set in order, this building of the earthly city, is not something which concerns only those who are following Christ; it concerns all men whatever creed they follow, whatever vocation they obey.

The message of Jesus goes farther.

He takes man who is part of the earthly city and says to him; "Remember the heavenly city which you must reach and from now on build up justice and love within yourself."

He sees man trapped by the limits of being a creature and destined for death, and he says: " 'I am the resurrection and the life' " (John 11:25).

He finds man aware, little by little, of his congenital insufficiency, which worries him and makes him suffer, and He says to him, "You are not only a son of man, you are a son of God: you are eternal. What is worrying you is your eternal sonship with the Father: what makes you unsatisfied and discontented is the divine life growing within you, which makes you see the limits of the frontiers of the visible, the human, the earthly."

Some people today get angry at hearing these things; some even interrupt Jesus and say, "If it's like that, keep your heaven; give us a more comfortable earth instead! You come on our side and help with the revolution; leave heaven to the sparrows, and we can dominate the earth."

And they might even be right. But Jesus is silent and waits for us to understand; He doesn't change.

He knows things we don't know. He knows that even when we have worked out the problems of the earthly city and given every man a house, a school, a hospital, freedom, and comfort, the last problem will still remain to be solved: death.

And it is not the easiest.

And it is not the smallest.

The gospel does not estrange men from the earth; it is not absent in the construction of human living; it doesn't get you out of doing things, living things, suffering things—but it goes beyond them.

It says what the Marxist would not know how to say, what the man of the earth would not be able to say.

On the evening of a social struggle in which believers and non-believers, Christians and non-Christians have found themselves fighting side by side for the triumph of justice, well-being, freedom, when others are silent because they no longer have anything to say, the Christian should begin speaking to proclaim in the name of Jesus a prophecy which always goes beyond the contingent, politics, time, and the relativity of human things.

What Jesus prophesies about the men who have wanted to follow Him concerns eternal life, which, although it begins here and has roots planted in human life, has its development in a reality beyond the earth, which He called Kingdom, and to which we are destined.

Of course this argument lends itself to misunderstandings.

Those who are not very familiar with the thought of Jesus, the escatological nature of human life and its eternal destiny, and who keep their eye on the dimensions of the earthly city with its justice and its limits, cry out before this vision and cannot accept it.

Sometimes even Christians search to bend the gospel message to their wills, search to find in it justification for saying that Jesus was a revolutionary, even violent.

That is what they often say, even at the Eucharistic gathering.

The spirit of Marxism, which is a radical earthly theory, has caught many unwary and spiritually unprepared Christians.

That is nothing to be surprised at.

The spirit of the times is always the best teacher, and it is difficult to get away from it.

Did the Christians of yesterday flee the spirit of their times, which was the spirit of the bourgeoisie?

Did the Christians of the day before yesterday flee the spirit of their times, which was colonialism?

Did the Christians of the Middle Ages flee the spirit of their times, which was feudalism?

And did the Christians of Constantine's time flee the spirit of their times, which was based on anything but the evangelical poverty of the Church?

The temptation to identify the Christian message with the culture of the times, with the sociology of the times, with the taste of the times is always very strong and is always under attack by the spiritual vanguard of the gospel.

For the gospel is not a culture, not a philosophy, not

a sociology, not a political system, and it can never be identified with them.

The nucleus of the gospel is incomprehensible within the framework of man's culture; it always goes further.

If you identify it with something of yours you fossilize it, institutionalize it, sterilize it, and, in the end, you cause it to die with your times.

Isn't that, perhaps, what we have seen at the Council?

Did this great, truly divine assembly of the people of God perhaps not have to use force to root out from the Church the stiffened, unbending positions of the spirit of dead times? Cast off the fetters of wanting to identify the gospel with the political, cultural, and philosophical visions of one time?

And now?

Now we are running the risk of making the same mistakes as we did in the past, going back to the beginning, transforming our vanguard into angry groups of pseudo-Marxists with a worthless facade of Christianity and a priest's cassock in the center.

Truly we lack prophecy.

And our inventiveness, our creativity, has been so badly reduced that we "sons of God" have to beg inspiration from the sons of men; we think the gospel is the only thing which is really new in the world!

Well, if you want to go in for politics, then get on with it! If you want to stir up a violent revolution, then stir it up! But don't do so under the name of Christ, because you will be using His name and His intention falsely.

It is true that Christ is a revolutionary, it is true that

144

He is violent, but not against others, only against Himself.

It is too easy to kill others, it is so difficult to die to oneself.

The violence of Christ is the Cross; it is planted in His heart, not in the hearts of His adversaries.

The violence of Jesus is deep love, not the sword or the prison, which is how we always want to resolve the problems which seem insoluable to us.

"Come on, let's bash a few hundred heads in, and everything will work out. . . ."

And then? . . . And then?

Afterwards perhaps the world will see rise up from the files of the same revolutionaries the dictators of the future, the egoists of the future, the bullies of the future, the torturers of the future?

It is discouraging to see how the greatest social revolutions have ended. It could be argued they have taught man nothing; he always wants to start back at the beginning.

No, it is not other people who need to be revolutionized, it is ourselves.

Jesus is the only revolutionary who sees things right, because He is not preoccupied with changing structures, but with changing men.

The structures renew themselves infinitely, but they are always oppressive as long as they are in the hands of man who is oppressive.

In vain does a poor man pass from one government to another, from one system to another, if there is no change in those who direct the government, or create the system.

Never has freedom been talked about so much, and

145

yet never have crueller systems for the crushing of freedom been established, including Communism, which I have always been drawn to as a Utopia, but which I have always seen collapse into an earthly history of oppression into which it would never have foreseen itself falling.

When we reread the text of the Twentieth Congress of the Russian Communist Party—that text which was such an honor to Khrushchev who had the courage to proclaim it—we cannot fail to hear the umpteenth confirmation of how incapable man is of seeing clearly into his own heart.

The Russian heart that had led such pure and courageous revolutionaries was the same heart that had sent tens of thousands of men before the firing squad, men who were thirsty for justice and had been condemned by tribunals so false and debased that poor mankind in all his history had never seen the like.

And that was the fruit of the most decisive and the most radical human revolution for centuries.

That is why Jesus revolutionizes hearts and not systems.

He wants to change the heart of man, not the laws, which were already quite good in antiquity.

That is how Jesus is a revolutionary, the only One who sees things right.

His revolution is slower, but it goes down deeper.

Above all it has no victims, and if it causes tears, they are only tears of penitence for one's own misdeeds, and for one's own incapacity to live out his own revolution.

But when it comes to the point of conquering hearts, the revolution of Jesus is total.

It is like kindly rain on thirsty fields, like sun on the frozen earth, like air in one's lungs, like bread on the table, like peace in the house. The revolution of the heart: that is the revolution of Jesus.

And this is where the greatest misunderstanding arises.

To speak of the revolution of the heart in an assembly of wolves (which men are, as Seneca pointed out) is like speaking of virginity in a whorehouse or penance during an orgy.

Indeed, it was in just such an absurdity that the trial of Jesus and His condemnation to death took place.

Often in such a situation the Christian who has no desire to pass for a fool—as Jesus did—opts out of the struggle; consciously or not, he allows himself to be taken in by the always alienating temptation of Ecclesiastes: "Vanity of vanities! All things are vanity!" (Eccl. 1:2).

He justifies his flight and his silence with religion itself and uses eschatology as a magic reply to the worrying "whys" of life.

Then people frame all kinds of theories and attempt to make fine distinctions: Should the Church enter politics or not? What is the role of the laity, the function of the hierarchy? These are all tricks to escape responsibility when it is costly, all excuses to give the poor so they can repeat to us that religion is the opiate of the people.

Raniero La Valle, in my opinion one of the most "Christian" Christians of our day, had two really inspired things to say about the problem of the Church and politics: "God is in the center, and not in any one part," and "if religion is the relationship with God in faith and this God has made a decision on man's behalf, then this religion is like the meridian which crosses all the parallels."

It is difficult to find a better way of describing the meeting point between the visible and the Invisible, between action and contemplation, between the life of religion and the life of politics, between the world and the Church.

The Christian cannot absent himself, the Church cannot remain silent if they truly want to take on man's problems and guard them in faith.

Eschatology, which is the entry into the kingdom, the realization of the kingdom, does not happen all in a flash and once-for-all at the end of history. Rather it is happening every day, at every instant in which the man who believes in the living Word, Jesus, turns it into reality by faith, by hope and by charity so he is vitally united to God.

The kingdom is already within us, even if it has yet to come in its fullness; every action of our existence, lived out as citizens of this invisible kingdom and accepted as a burning demand of the gospel, reinforces its structure and widens its boundaries.

The Christian is thus at the center of things, there where his God is; with the meridian of his faith he must cut through all the parallels of the life of man.

But speaking in the name of his God he prophesies; he does not discuss political technicalities. Seeking to save man, to free man, he acts out of love, not out of political good sense or historical culture.

Jeremiah was a terrible politician, and after any speech of his about what was going to happen in Israel's politics, he always ended up in prison.

But he was a prophet: the light of his words, which came down from Another, cast light on all the politics which Israel should have been concerned with for her salvation.

When the man of God speaks, when the Church—the society of faith and grace speaks—there is no need for aesthetics, for technology, for culture. Prophecy, being divine by nature, has the power of casting light on man's march towards freedom; charity, having its origin in the theological love of God, has an exact vision of things and knows what is really good for man.

And let us remember: what is good for man always comes to the light of history screened by three unequivocal words: life, light, love. These are the same words which indicate the Person of the Father, the Person of the Son, and the Person of the Holy Spirit.

Defending life, witnessing light, living out love; these remain forever and for every occasion the divine background of prophecy; they are the specific duty of anyone who calls upon God, following Christ's unmistakable example.

An assembly where people do not love each other, where they accuse each other, where there is rancor or hatred, cannot call itself prophetic.

A man who keeps silent about the truth, who hides the light, is not a prophet.

A people which kills, which deteriorates the quality of life, which suffocates the poor, which is not free, is not a prophetic people.

That is why it is not enough for just any assembly to call itself Church, just as it is not enough to be a bishop or a pope in order to possess prophecy.

A group of young people which meets for sports or

outings with the "do everything" blessing of the up-to-date parish, another group which meets to camouflage some political position cannot be called Church, even if the sports are refereed by a famous devout layman and the social ideas are worked out by a priest.

To call itself Church, an assembly must mirror the first assembly that met in the Upper Room with Christ: an assembly of faith and grace, an assembly of love and Eucharist, an assembly of prayer and prophecy.

But it is not easy to prophesy; it is terribly costly. It has to be drawn from the silence of God, and there is need to swim against the stream, need to pray at length, need to be without fear.

That is when we get to doing other things, cheating at the game or copying everyone else, as long as we don't seem useless or out-of-date.

Then there is public opinion, which takes on the job of leveling everything, filing everything, regulating everything.

How easy for the Christian to become dominated by public opinion!

It can even be heard in the Sunday morning sermon.

When I was young, nationalism was "in"; in many sermons I heard there were pleas to give gold for our native land, thus greeting the dawn of a new empire with a patriotic tear.

Now I am old, different things are in, and I see priests with studiously untidy habits according to the canons of aesthetic poverty, trying to show the young that if the bourgeois priests of another time made mistaken choices, here they are to make the right ones at last.

Christians without prophecy, and moreover, without imagination!

Poor Jesus! How you have been abandoned!

Worse: how falsely You have been presented!

CHAPTER XVI

"If I . . . have not love, I am nothing."
(1 Cor. 13:2)

What does it mean, "a revolution of the heart," a change of heart?

That is precisely the territory of Jesus, what the real gospel is all about.

But do our hearts need changing?

Anyone of you who feels right in his heart, on good terms with his own heart, satisfied with his own heart, raise your hand. I certainly shall not put up mine.

Nothing has made me suffer so much as my heart!

Nothing in my life has rewarded me with heavier chains!

Even today, after so many years of forcing myself, of renunciations, of battles, it is like a sickness within me.

If I could tear it out, I should do so willingly, but I cannot. I must not.

There is nothing to be done: I must force myself to

change it. I have been trying for so many years and I have not succeeded yet.

By way of encouragement, God tells me in scripture: "I will remove the stony heart from their bodies, and replace it with a natural heart . . ." (Ezek. 11:19). But I'm still waiting, asking myself when and how this will happen.

In our community the other day there wasn't much coffee.

Coffee does me good down here in the desert . . . it helps me . . . I am old.

I was worried about not having any, about spending a few hours feeling dull and weak, and so—without perceiving the evil I was doing—I went into the kitchen before the others and drank up all that was left.

Afterwards, having suffered all day and made my confession, I thought in shame of my selfishness, of the ease with which I had excluded my two brothers from those black, bitter remains.

It seems a tiny thing, yet in that cup of coffee, taken and not shared with my brothers, is the root of all the evil which disturbs us, the poison of all the arrogance which selfishness, riches, and power create.

The difference between me and Jesus is right here, in an affair that seems simple but isn't at all; after a whole life time it is still there to make you think. Jesus would have left the coffee for His brothers; I excluded my brothers.

No, it isn't easy to live with hearts like ours: let us confess it.

Let us look, for example, at what happens in marital love.

When a man says to a woman, "I love you," his first impression is that he really wants good for her.

But before long he realizes that in reality it is himself he loves, and then, too often, selfishness poisons the relationship and reduces it to an act of possession, rather than a gift of oneself.

How difficult it is to love!

I have no doubts in stating that in a hundred acts which we believe to be acts of love, the highest percentage are performed out of pure selfishness, out of turning in on oneself, out of search for pleasure for its own sake, out of arrogance.

That is why love goes into crisis, transforming itself into acts which mortify us and divide us.

That is *eros* feeding upon one another, attempting to tear from life just one drop of pleasure by way of the other. It is the transformation of love into a drug.

With what result?

The destruction of everything, the pollution of everything.

Oh, if such behavior at least made us happy; if by drugging ourselves we could find peace, joy, fullness!

But God knows where this blundering road is leading.

There is no sorrow greater than love betrayed by pleasure!

It is this sorrow which shapes the basis of our relationships and the infinite boredom of our sick existence.

Well, in the middle of this misery of ours, something grafts the divine life into us, something sets in motion the announcement of salvation, the good news of peace and resurrection.

By ourselves we are not capable of love. God, who

154

comes to us as presence, as grace, as eternal life teaches us to love.

The mystery revealed to us by Christ is not only love between two; it is love between three. *Eros* is transformed into *agape,* the couple is transformed into a family, human love is transformed into a banquet.

God's way of living love, by charity, is the solution to the problem of our poor love.

The true novelty of Christianity is the triune love of God in us, which is the perfect way of loving. This is eternal life: it is God's way of loving in us, a way of bringing us into the kingdom little by little, of freeing us from the destruction of selfishness, of making our love gratuitous, of introducing the gift of self into the never-ended dream of possessing someone or something. Renunciation becomes a true witness to life.

Love between two—bridegroom and bride, friend and friend, brother and brother, mother and son—always runs the risk of becoming exclusive, possessive, motivated by self-interest, introversion, sensuality.

Charity, which is God's way of loving, corrects this tension, introduces a third element to catalize self-interest, turning it towards generosity and the gratuitous gift of oneself. Then love is truly universal.

A married couple who only love each other end by becoming egotistic, closed in; little by little, their love dries up. If they introduce charity, which is the triune way of loving, they find in their union an ever-new fountain of freshness, a corrective to sensuality, an ideal reference which carries them outside themselves into an authentically divine dimension.

Acceptance of a child—what is it if not concrete acceptance of the third person, present in their love, which will help them to come out from their potential egotism and will even drag sensuality—always as dangerous as a drug—towards poetry of fecundity and life?

And it is the same for any other relationship of love, between men or between men and things.

Human love tends to bring about a love between two; charity teaches us to keep sight of the third presence.

Oh, I know these are only images, but even images are useful! God in His love is Trinity, and love is the image, even though pale and inadequate, of the Trinity.

The bridegroom who loves the bride is a person; the bride who gazes on the bridegroom and loves him is the other person. Love which runs the risk of drying up with each feeding on the other, in pleasure which is an end in itself, becomes free, becomes godlike, when the eyes of the child appear between the two—the personification of the love between the two.

And so it is in all relationships.

The danger of making love sterile through the selfishness of pleasure disappears, or at least diminishes, if one introduces into the relationship an ideal element, an aim, a dynamic, something which causes man to rise above the terrible danger of reducing the relationship into a single moment of pleasure.

Because, don't let us forget, nothing is more destructive than pleasure sought for its own sake.

Nothing weakens man more than the sensual search for pleasure. Imperial power itself falls before the use and abuse of this refined poison known to all the civilizations of the welfare state.

There is no further ideal when we become slaves to

it; there is no limit to our own ruin when we become entangled in it.

Oh, if, as I said before, this pleasure at least created peace, joy . . . then let it come! Who could deny it? But we know what it creates. What sadness a man gets from the cult of pleasure!

What chains it places upon the shoulders of these stupified drug addicts.

No, there is no peace for anyone who leaves the equilibrium created by nature itself. I think there is less suffering in crucifixion than in being drugged. If there is a hell on earth, and there is, it is more for those who have scarched out pleasure without regard for law and affections, than for those who have accepted daily suffering and the cross of existence.

If it were not so, God would not be God.

Human love is a straight line, the union of two points in the space of the creature.

Charity is a triangle.

The "revolution of the heart" is this: to transform the straight lines of our loves into triangles, with the triune presence of God at the vertex.

This presence of God in our love and the acceptation of all its demands is the salvation, the sublimation of our love.

Love becomes charity.

Time becomes eternity.

The heart of man becomes the heart of Christ.

That is why St. Paul says that love is not enough, and that if there is no charity I am nothing.

His hymn to this kind of love—charity—should be learned by heart.

If I speak with human tongues and angelic as well, but do not have love, I am a noisy gong, a clanging cymbal. If I have the gift of prophecy and, with full knowledge, comprehend all mysteries, if I have faith great enough to move mountains, but have not love, I am nothing. If I give everything I have to feed the poor and hand over my body to be burned, but have not love, I gain nothing.

Love is patient; love is kind. Love is not jealous, it does not put on airs, it is not snobbish. Love is never rude, it is not self-seeking, it is not prone to anger; neither does it brood over injuries. Love does not rejoice in what is wrong but rejoices with the truth. There is no limit to love's forbearance, to its trust, its hope, its power to endure.

Love never fails. Prophecies will cease, tongues will be silent, knowledge will pass away. Our knowledge is imperfect and our prophesying is imperfect. When the perfect comes, the imperfect will pass away. When I was a child I used to talk like a child, think like a child, reason like a child. When I became a man I put childish ways aside. Now we see indistinctly, as in a mirror; then we shall see face to face. My knowledge is imperfect now; then I shall know even as I am known. There are in the end three things that last: faith, hope and love, and the greatest of these is love. (1 Cor. 13:1-13)

No, it is not enough to give and to act to resolve our problems! Because even by giving and acting I can do harm, or at least I can do something that serves no purpose. Let us not forget this challenging quotation from St. Paul: "If I give everything I have to feed the poor and hand over my body to be burned, but have not love, I gain nothing."

This quotation should be written on the facade of many of our Christian institutions and, even more so, in the notes of the so-called religious activists.

CHAPTER XVII

"You will all come to the same end unless you reform." (Luke 13:5)

Without any doubt, one of the most dangerous enemies man has to combat in the spiritual life is pleasure. Notice I say pleasure, not joy or happiness; I say pleasure, not exultance or the fullness of being.

Pleasure, that alluring and mysterious sensation, cradled in the senses and the spirit, and arching towards a clearly defined end, is in nature a creation of God's.

Yes, it is a creation of God's!

Very tiny, very sweet, very easy, sympathetic and convivial as can be, penetrating and intrusive as can be, God placed it in our senses to help them come to fullness, to express themselves, to live.

I would say more: to do His holy will.

Pleasure urges man, almost without his realizing it, to do things which are indispensable for life, through an impression of fullness, truth, and joy inherent in his own existence.

The pleasure of food and drink helps man to nourish himself; the pleasure of sleep to concede fatigue a proper period of rest; the pleasure of possession gives him the sense of his kingship over the universe; the pleasure of self-evaluation, the sense of human dignity; the pleasure of friendship, the joy of relationships and the unsuppressable sense of man's socialability.

What are we to say then of the pleasure of sex?

It presides at nothing less than the mystery of life and has been placed in us by God to make us carry out His own creative joy and exultation.

Up to this point, no comment. On the contrary this little creation, pleasure, is to be highly praised, for it can make agreeable and joyful a heavy and rhythmical waste of time, such as eating food. And it makes terribly attractive a task so awesome as becoming fathers and mothers.

Where is the evil then?

Why should this little creation, which is so attractive and so beneficial, be dangerous?

Yes, it is dangerous, just because it is so attractive, and it is even more dangerous because we are so weak in letting ourselves be attracted.

I should say that this power of attraction, added to our weakness in letting ourselves be attracted, creates a dangerous disequilibrium, which ends, sooner or later, by doing us harm.

In old-fashioned language that is called sin.

St. Augustine called it disorder.

Today, we moderns willingly call it exaggeration.

In fact:

Exaggeration in eating can be called greed.

Exaggeration in sleep can be called laziness or sloth.

Exaggeration in self-esteem can be called pride.

Exaggeration in feelings, envy or jealousy.

Exaggeration in love of possession, avarice.

And exaggeration in the search for sexual pleasure, lust.

Make the list out properly and there are the deadly sins; make out the synthesis and you have the pleasure which today is called "drugs."

To drug oneself means letting oneself be dominated by aimless pleasure; it means seeking pleasure in the pure state, detaching from the motives for which God handed it to us, isolating it from the purpose for which it was created and put into us as a bridge between thought and action, between duty and its fulfillment.

To drug oneself means abasing this creature of God called pleasure, it means making an instrument of this serene and carefree child that the creativity of God handed us so we might enjoy life more easily and walk more promptly towards His divine will.

Is not the indolence of young people, lolling around without constructive goals, a way of drugging oneself into nothingness?

Is not using a man or woman in order to squeeze out one drop of pleasure a way of drugging of oneself with sensuality and libido?

Is not injecting any kind of stimulant into one's blood or smoking opium a perversion?

Yes, a perversion!

It is a perversion because it is against nature.

It is a perversion because it is pure selfishness.

It is a perversion because it is death.

It is a perversion because it is an exploitation of the human creature, as prostitution is an exploitation of creation, and miserly possession an exploitation of dominion.

And even those who are partaking in these things know that these are perversions. Indeed, they try to hide them. "Men loved the darkness better than light because their deeds were wicked" (John 3:19).

Just as the young man who drugs himself tries to hide, so the man who tries to manipulate the scales of society or gets into the smeared politics of power or of war tries to hide. " 'Be on your guard against false prophets who come to you in sheep's clothing but underneath are wolves on the prowl. You will know them by their deeds' " (Matthew 7:15-16).

The first sign that perversion is a turning off the road, that sin is harmful, that drugging oneself leads to death, is sadness.

Nature is relentless and strikes anyone who acts against her. At once.

How bitter the drug addict's awakening!

What infinite unhappiness the dawn holds for anyone who prostitutes himself or uses a prostitute!

What anxiety the perverts and the sensualists go through!

Today, to comfort themselves, people say: "That's not sin, it's like drinking a glass of water, it's one of nature's demands . . ."

Well, then why do you come to me secretly, to ask if it's all right?

Why don't you get on with it without asking questions?

Because the first warning for anyone walking in error

comes from within, from that presence which they called conscience in the old days.

"I don't know why, but there's something wrong. I laugh, but I'm so sad! I sing in order to forget, but I feel as though I were in a cave alone. . . . I am enclosed in my selfishness and I can't stand any more. . . . I have everything I want at home, yet I'm no longer capable of love and conversation."

Yes, the first call comes from within, and it is reliable because it is continual, inexorable, dull, subtle.

For one moment of pleasure, twenty-four hours of misery; for the brief exploitation of a friend, so much undefined boredom. And then, it's not easy to stop. This is the most dangerous point, because exaggeration becomes ever greater exaggeration—especially today, when we are no longer used to resisting, and when the great means at our disposal accelerate the absorbing process of pleasure and the inexorable fall into the dark well of eroticism, drugs, perversion.

Do you want a picture of it?

It is not of today, because it was already described in the psalms, but it is always up-to-date.

> *Oh Lord, in your anger punish me not*
> *in your wrath chastise me not;*
> *For your arrows have sunk deep in me,*
> *and your hand has come down upon me.*
> *There is no health in my flesh because of*
> *your indignation;*
> *there is no wholesomeness in my bones because*
> *of my sin,*
> *For my iniquities have overwhelmed me;*

164

> they are like a heavy burden, beyond my
>   strength.
> Noisome and festering are my sores
>   because of my folly,
> I am stooped and bowed down profoundly;
>   all the day I go in mourning,
> For my loins are filled with burning pains;
>   there is no health in my flesh.
> I am numbed and severely crushed;
>   I roar with anguish of heart.

(Ps. 38:2-9)

No, sin is not interesting; it is so very boring. And it is boring because deep down it is an act of selfishness, pure selfishness.

And this act occurs in our human nature, which, although poor, is made for the complete opposite of selfishness.

Man is made for the gift of himself.

Man is happy only when he has given himself.

The things which are truly ours are the things we have given.

Selfishness makes us unhappy; a love which gives makes us happy.

The difference between the chaste embrace of a married couple and the embrace of a prostitute is right here. The former is liberating because it is the gift of self, the latter is humiliating because it is selfishness. The former brings joy, the latter leaves a bad taste in your mouth.

It is always that way.

If you give yourself you are happy; if you exploit your brother or what is his, you are unhappy.

I would say that the meaning of the universe as a whole is found in the Eucharist, the free gift of God to man and man to God. The obverse of this meaning is found in sin, the turning in of man upon himself and the seed that flowers in death.

For sin begets death, and hell is its home.

We need not ask ourselves: Does hell exist?

We need only ask: Where does sin have its home?, and we will see and taste hell.

The man who is in sin is already in hell. Your hell is conditional as long as you can drag yourself out of it; it is permanent when you are helpless to emerge.

Come out, while you are still able!

But be afraid indeed of the awful possibility that lurks for us of "not being able any longer to come forth."

The prodigal son dragged himself out in time (cf. Luke 15:11-32); the rich man at his feast was no longer able (cf. Luke 16:19-30).

Jesus speaks the terrible words: "You will all come to the same end unless you reform" (Luke 13:3). The words are all the more fearful coming from the lips of one who is so patient and humble of heart.

His words betray a deep apprehensiveness that preoccupied him; we cannot afford to joke about what he says. We are faced here with irremediable destruction.

That is what frightens me.

How could the rich man "who dressed in purple and linen and feasted splendidly every day" (Luke 16:19) have become so depraved that he was no longer able to recognize behind the appearance of the suffering Lazarus the God of love who was testing him in love and, having found him cold, was "spewing him out of his mouth" (cf. Rev. 3:16)?

How can an addict reach the point of striking his own mother in order to get money for his habit?

How can a man kill a brother who stands in the way of his desires?

How can men tear down ideals, feelings, family, and health just to continue on such depraved paths?

It's easy to say: Hell can't exist, because God is good! But what of the man who is already in hell, hurled into it by the full perversity of his own will?

Isn't a society a hell when it's based on money, lust, and debauchery?

Isn't the world of the addict a hell?

Isn't war a hell when it's waged solely to crush the weak, rob the poor, and increase one's own power?

Isn't family life a hell when it's filled with hatred and no one communicates any more?

Isn't sexual love a hell when it is transformed into pure carnal desire?

Hell is a state; it is a reality we build with our own hands and our own evil desires.

The only real problem left concerning hell is its permanence. But to understand that is beyond the power of reason, for we do not live in the dimension of eternity and so cannot grasp it.

But we can believe in or reject the eternity of hell, depending on whether we live by the power of faith, just as faith determines whether or not God exists, whether or not Jesus is present in the Eucharist, whether or not there will be a resurrection at the end of time.

In any event I think it behooves us to accept and try

to apply Jesus' words: "You will all come to the same end unless you reform."

But what does it mean to "reform" or "repent"?

In biblical language to repent means "to proceed against," "to swim against the current," "to resist the evil one," "to establish the conditions needed for overcoming oneself."

Repentance, then, is within our power, even if we feel no desire for it and are tempted to put off dealing with the problem.

To begin with, we must go against the ideas of the day, for these are always opposed to the gospel. We must resist "the latest fashion and the spirit of the times," which are almost always influenced by the evil one.

Today people say: "Sex really isn't such a problem after all. We ought to stop worrying about it, as we have the other taboos. What's wrong with sex? Tell me: what's wrong with it? Do you find nudity distasteful? Does it obsess you? If so, look the problem in the face and you'll get rid of your obsession. Break through the prison bars of your outmoded morality and just live in accordance with nature. Why do you always see evil where there's only love?"

It doesn't take much experience to understand what can happen in a society where this kind of liberating talk prevails.

It won't take long for a man to find that every night he's ready for a new love. Everyone's bed will welcome people more like prostitutes, male or female, than spouses who find peace in their sweet self-giving.

No! We have reached the point in our pagan civilization when we can no longer compromise with the "spirit of the times" and the accepted ideas of our age.

That spirit is genuinely diabolical; those ideas are genuinely destructive.

What will you say to a poor young fellow who has become disillusioned and let himself be trapped by drugs? "Go and take some more drugs!"?

"Do you want to be freed from your obsession with nudity? Go and look at pornographic magazines."!

I know perfectly well that this path will never lead to freedom. So, if I want freedom I must swim against the current; I must tear myself away and flee.

We are in a terrifying situation, and that is the one thing that can almost make us despair.

Our western civilization is being drowned in sensual and erotic pleasure.

Young people are destroying themselves with drugs, sex, and idleness, and a civilization that now lacks any authentic, lasting ideals looks on with a stupid smile!

The older generation, bigoted and neck-deep in compromise, wastes its time defending itself by passing laws against divorce, instead of bearing witness, out of deep faith, to the certainty of the gospel and the light that a true and freely given love always brings.

Never before, in my view, has Jesus' dramatic warning been so appropriate: "You will all come to the same end unless you reform."

Never before, in my view, has it been so necessary as today to discipline the flesh and make it submissive to the spirit.

Never before has there been such a time for taking the pilgrim's pouch and a little hard bread and going the weary way of penitence. Only there will our body, the temple of God, recover its lightsomeness.

I want no one to grow discouraged as he travels the hard road of repentance. So I would like to suggest to those who feel weak a secret, the true secret.

"Do not rely on your own courage and your own strength of will. Rely rather on your prayer. Regard one thing as certain: 'Virtue does not give rise to true prayer; prayer gives rise to true virtue.' "

The strength of man by himself does not amount to much, even though it is necessary.

What is really important is the encounter between man's strength and God who comes to him; that encounter comes to pass through man's prayer.

Here again, then, our hope is in "God who comes!"

The man who can cry out and lament and pray is the one who may expect the power of the God who comes, supporting him at the moment of his greatest weakness.

Victory comes out of that encounter.

This is why at death's door we who hope securely in the resurrection will cry out of our total poverty: "Come, Lord! Come quickly!" This is why, when faced with our own weakness as we admit the need of repentance, we cry out with the same strength of spirit: "Come, Lord Jesus!" (Rev. 22:20).

CHAPTER XVIII

" 'You shall love the Lord your God with all your heart, with all your soul, with all your strength, and with all your mind; and your neighbor as yourself,' " (Luke 10:27)

In our day, as soon as you speak about the mystery of prayer, people cry, Prayer! There is no time for prayer! All those people to feed, all those real things to organize, how can you still ask us to waste our precious time?

"Why search for a hypothetical relationship with the invisible God, when you can find the immediate and concrete in visible man?

"And man is the visible presence of God on earth: serve him, save him, and you've done it all!"

And what can we say when this stand is taken not least by the witnesses of the invisible God, by priests and religious? "Brother Carlo, you are speaking of the desert, of silence, of prayer. But how can you talk like that to us, when we are up to our necks in contemporary civilization, snowed under by thousands and thousands of tasks, caught up from morning to night in contacts with men and the service of the poor?" And you keep silence with a compassionate smile and with the security of a man who continues to believe firmly in past prejudices.

But the fact is that they are not past prejudices!

The fact is that the priest who says he no longer has time to pray will be found on a painful search for his identity after a few years. The busy militant who has so little time that he can't waste time praying, will be found so empty in a few years that you won't know what to do to give him back a little faith in the ideal he has been wanting to serve until now.

No, these are not prejudices.

The first commandment remains the first commandment, and it is the *first*—both under the old law (cf. Deut. 6:5) and under the new (cf. Luke 12:30) that was pronounced by Jesus—"You shall love the Lord your God with all your heart, with all your soul, with all your strength, and with all your mind; and your neighbor as yourself" (Luke 10:27).

Moreover, it is hammered in so forcefully that it leaves no doubts. It would seem that no part of man has been forgotten on the list—heart, soul, mind, strength—in order to emphasize the necessity of decision in loving God!

And then?

And then the problem. If you don't pray, if you are not searching for a personal relationship with God, if you don't stay with Him for long periods in order to know Him, study Him, understand Him, little by little you will start forgetting Him, your memory will weaken, you will no longer recognize Him. You will not be able to, because you will no longer know how to love.

The proverb "Out of sight out of mind" is true not only about men; it is terribly true about God, too.

Take an example.

If a fiancé telephones his fiancée to tell her, "I'm sorry, this evening I can't come, I've so much work!", there is nothing wrong. But if it is the thousandth time he has made the same call, he has not been to see her in weeks on the excuse of work or outings with his friends, it is more serious—rather, it is quite clear: this is not love.

Because the lover is capable of overcoming all difficulties and discovering all the stratagems necessary to meet his soul's beloved.

So it is better to get clear with ourselves what our relationship with God is.

Have you been not praying, not seeking Him personally because you don't love Him, or because you have no time?

Usually we are afraid to accept the first reality; it is easier to fix on the second.

This is the true problem, which we do not try to resolve because our minds are confused.

And there is a complex of things which help confuse thought: it is not all our fault.

We are terribly conditioned by our times, and it is so difficult to escape this conditioning.

Bombarded from morning to night not only by the consumer society but, worse, by the noisy society, the slogans, the sensuality, the self-assurance of man, how can we avoid being influenced by them?

173

The visible has become so thick that it leaves no space for the invisible.

Pop heroes and sports heroes have been thrust at your over-excited mind so that they leave no space in your living room for the heroes of the bible who were with you in the past.

The very figure of Jesus begins to fade in your heart; after three hours before the television screen of this world, you barely hear Him saying anything to you.

It is hard to face, but that is how it is.

Well, what is the difference between Peter walking the roads of the Empire, urged on solely by the passionate love for Jesus which filled his heart and mind and made him succumb to the depths of such a love, and you, who no longer feel the living presence of the divine Master, and no longer even know where He lives?

Then we come to the question, "Why did I become a priest?", "Why did I enter this convent?". "Why go on trying to be a good Christian?".

And the answer will not come—rather we are afraid of giving it.

Since one cannot live without love, and since there has been a wasting away of your love for a personal God—which means love for the person of Jesus, love for the person of the Father, love for the person of the Holy Spirit—you have been forced to find other loves as substitutes.

It would have happened to Peter and Paul, too, if they had not known how to cultivate a passionate love of Jesus; instead of dying as martyrs and giving us the eternal witness of their well-spent lives, they would have died amid the ruins of their lost vocations.

Now I should like to say a word to anyone who has the heart of a militant, an activist, who has always had the impression that to pray is to run the risk of alienation from our brothers and their troubles.

This point of view is not completely wrong, I know. In the past too many people gave the impression of a Christianity which was other-worldly, absent. Today's thirst is for concreteness and reality, I know. But listen to this simple, linear testimony:

Here in Beni-Abbes, during the winter, nomads often arrive with their tents.

They are the poorest of men: they no longer have any camels or goats to sell, no longer the strength to organize caravans. They are seeking some place they can be helped to settle down into a new social reality which has no further need for the nomadic life.

One day a French woman, who was making a retreat here, was walking beside one of these tents. She stopped to pass the time of day and, as she did so, realized that a Tuareg girl, thin as a rake, was trembling with cold.

It is strange, but that is how it is: in the desert it is cold in the sunless dawns.

"Why don't you cover yourself up?", she asked.

"Because I've nothing to cover myself with," replied the girl.

The French woman, without going to the roots of the problem, went—to pray.

She entered the hermitage built by Pére de Foucauld himself, where the Blessed Sacrament is exposed.

She prostrated herself in the sand before Jesus, present under the sign of faith, "the Eucharist."

Some time passed, she sought contact with the Eternal One, she tried to pray.

"I couldn't go on," she told me afterwards. "I couldn't pray. I had to go out, back to the tent, and give that child one of my sweaters. Then I returned, and then I was able to pray."

Here is what I should like to say to those who are afraid of personal prayer with God, who don't want to alienate themselves from their suffering brethren.

If you pray, if you pray seriously, if you pray in truth, it will be God Himself who will send you out, with greater strength, with greater love, towards your brothers, so that you may love them more gratuitously and serve them more delicately.

Well then, you will say, why, why in the past have too many Christians scandalized me with their indifference, with the hardness of their bigoted hearts, with the hermetic sealing of themselves against every problem of justice and liberation of the people?

Yet they were praying, they were contemplating!

No, if they were praying, their prayer was just a bit of rhetoric. If they were contemplating, they were contemplating . . . nothing.

They were deceiving you, and they were deceiving the Church.

It is impossible to pray to a personal God—that is, love a personal God—and remain indifferent to your suffering brethren.

It is impossible.

Anyone who prays without suffering for his suffering brothers is praying to a pole, a shadow, not to the living God.

Because if you pray to the living God, you who are

176

living, He, the Living One, sends you to your living brothers.

If you pray to the living God, your prayer passes through the heart of Christ Crucified, the only model of the way we must love the Father and our brothers, the point of convergence between the vertical dimension of the Absolute and the horizontal dimension of all mankind needing salvation.

After Christ it is no longer possible to separate the love of the Father from the love of our brothers.

If you begin by loving your brothers, keep well in mind that you cannot separate this love from love for the Father.

The Father is a person—and He has a right to be loved, just as your brothers have a right to be loved.

And persons are loved for themselves, not for other ends.

To love someone and use him for other ends means, in poor words, to exploit him, and today everybody agrees that this must not happen.

And if we agree not to exploit man, why should we end by exploiting God?

So you cannot say "By loving my brothers I love the Father," just as you cannot say "By loving the Father, I love my brothers."

You must love the Father, and you must love your brothers, every one of them.

Love is personal, and it is strong and tenacious only if it is personal.

You cannot say "I love Christ present in the assembly of the brothers," if you do not first love Christ in Himself as person, as son.

It is certain that the mystical Christ, which is the

Church, is to be loved in His mysterious presence in the people of God, but there also exists the person of Christ, who must be loved passionately.

There also exists the person of the Holy Spirit who must be loved personally with all your strength, with all your heart, with all your self.

And that is what the first commandment means.

But we are coming to the doing and the giving and the speaking out that preoccupy men in the Church today, and we ask ourselves, "What must I do?", "What must I give?", "What must I speak?".

Have you not realized that we do so many useless things?

That we give lifeless things?

That we say boring things which absolutely nobody listens to.

If I counted up all the hours consumed by Church organizations and futile meetings, I should almost reach infinity.

And what are we to say of the infinite boredom provoked in the assembled people of God by those who speak without conviction, without authenticity, without prophecy?

Where can I get conviction, if not in prolonged prayer?

Where can I get authenticity, if not in my personal experience of God?

Where can I get prophecy, if not the true giver of every prophecy, God Himself?

I know that if I do not pray, I am deaf, I am dumb, I am incapable of saying anything valid.

I know that if I do not seek the personal love of God, I am faltering and weak in my actions.

I know that if I do not contemplate, I am without prophecy, without heaven, without newness.

God has always revealed Himself to me as "newness," as He who is eternally new and able to renew things. Well, it is only in the contemplation of His face that I am able to find the right word to say to my brothers.

They are not seeking culture or technology or politics or art or science from me. They are seeking the word of prophecy which will help them enter the kingdom.

That word is possessed only by God, and God gives it to whoever is searching for it, not to someone who says he has no time to stay with Him.

Saying "I've no time to pray because I've so much to do" is like saying: "I don't know God, but I want to speak on Him."

"I've lost sight of Him, but I want to show you where He is to be found."

These things happen, but they are not logical, and they give witness to our lack of logic.

But there is something greater, more abysmal than our lack of logic in dealing with God.

Try to think about it.

CHAPTER XIX

" 'You are Peter and on this rock ...' "
(Matt. 16:18)

How baffling you are, oh Church, and yet how I love you!

How you have made me suffer, and yet how much I owe you!

I should like to see you destroyed, and yet I need your presence.

You have given me so much scandal and yet you have made me understand sanctity.

I have seen nothing in the world more devoted to obscurity, more compromised, more false, and I have touched nothing more pure, more generous, more beautiful. How often I have wanted to shut the doors of my soul in your face, and how often I have prayed to die in the safety of your arms.

No, I cannot free myself from you, because I am you, although not completely.

And where should I go?

180

To build myself another church?

But I could build one only with the same defects, because they are mine, defects which I have inside myself. And if I built one, it would be my church, no longer the Church of Christ.

I am old enough to understand that I am no better than other people.

The day before yesterday a friend wrote a letter to a newspaper, saying, "I am leaving the Church because, with the compromises she makes with the rich, I cannot believe in her."

It makes me unhappy.

Either he is sentimental and lacks experience, which I can forgive him; or else he is proud and believes he is better than other men, more credible than they are.

No one of us is credible so long as he is on this earth.

St. Francis cried out: "You believe I am a saint, but you do not know I could still have children by a prostitute if Christ did not sustain me."

Credibility does not belong to men, only to God and to Christ.

Only weakness belongs to man—and maybe good intentions of carrying out some good work, aided by the grace pouring out from the invisible veins of the visible Church.

Perhaps the Church of yesterday was better than that of today? Perhaps the Church of Jerusalem was more credible than the Christian churches today?

Paul arrived in Jerusalem, his powerful charismatic message carrying his deep thirst for universality, and heard the words of James about the foreskins which needed to be circumcized, and saw the weakness of Peter who was loitering with the rich men of his time (the sons of Abraham) and who gave scandal by dining only with the pure. Did this make him doubt the truth of the Church, which Christ had founded so fresh, or make him want to go off and found another at Antioch or Tarsus?

Catherine of Sienna saw that the pope was mixing—and how he was mixing—in the dirty politics against her city, the city of her heart. Did she think up the idea of going to the Siennese hills, transparent as the heavens, and making another church more transparent than the Roman one, which was so murky, so full of sins, so caught up in politics?

No, I do not believe so, because both Paul and Catherine knew how to distinguish between the persons who form the Church, "the personnel of the Church," as Maritain says, and this human society called Church, which unlike all other human groups has received from God a supernatural, holy, immaculate, pure, unfailing, infallible personality, loved as the bride of Christ and worthy of being loved by me as a sweet mother.

Here is the mystery of the Church of Christ, a true, impenetrable mystery.

She has the power to give me holiness, yet she is made up, all the way through, of sinners—and what sinners!

She has the omnipotent and invincible faith to renew the Eucharist, yet she is made up of weak men groping in the darkness and fighting daily against the temptation of losing their faith.

She carries a message of pure transparence, yet she is incarnate in a mess of dirt, which is the dirt of the world.

She speaks of the sweetness of the Master, of his nonviolence, yet in history she has sent armies to disembowel infidels and to torture heretics.

She carries a message of evangelical poverty, yet she often seeks gifts and alliances with the powerful.

We have only to read of the Inquisition trial of St. Joan of Arc to convince ourselves that Stalin was not the first to falsify charges and corrupt the judges.

We have only to consider what the innocent Galileo was made to sign under threats to be convinced that the men of the Church, the personnel of the Church, although they make up the Church, are often evil men and fallible personnel, capable of making errors as great as the earth's path round the sun.

It is useless to want anything else from the Church except this mystery of infallibility and fallibility, sanctity and sin, courage and weakness, credibility and the lack of it.

People who are dreaming of something different from this reality are simply wasting time and keep going back to the beginning again. Moreover, they show they have not understood man.

Because that is man, just as the Church shows him to be, in his wickedness and, at the same time, in his invincible courage, which faith in Christ has given him, and the love of Christ has him live.

When I was young I could not understand why Jesus, notwithstanding Peter's denial, wanted him as head, his successor, the first pope. Now I am no longer bewildered: I understand better and better how building the Church on the tomb of a traitor, a man who got frightened at the chattering of a servant-girl, was like a constant warning to keep every one of us humble and conscious of our own frailty.

No, I am not leaving the Church which was founded on such a weak rock, because I should found another on an even weaker rock.

And what do rocks matter anyway? What matters is the promise of Christ, the cement which holds the stones together, and that is the Holy Spirit. Only the Holy Spirit is capable of building the Church with such badly hewn stones as ourselves!

Only the Holy Spirit can hold us together, notwithstanding ourselves, notwithstanding the centrifugal force which is given us by our limitless pride.

When I hear the debate within the Church I am pleased. I take it as a serious, profound meditation, resulting from a thirst for good and a clear, free vision of things.

"We must be poor . . . evangelical . . . we must not believe in alliances with great powers . . . etc."

But, in the end, I feel that this debate, concerning my parish priest, my bishop, my pope, as persons, concerns me too, as a person, and I feel I am in the same boat, the same family, the blood-brother of matriculated sinners and a sinner myself.

That is when I go in for debate myself, and I realize how difficult conversion is.

Because it could be—and it happens—that while I am in the drawing room after a sumptuous dinner discussing the burning problems of Portuguese colonialism, I forget my wife or my mother all alone in the kitchen, washing the dishes from the feast with my sophisticated friends. Is the spirit of colonialism not at the bottom of our hearts?

Because maybe—and it happens—that at the same moment I am hurling myself furiously against the sins committed by the racist pride of whites against blacks, I find I am the kind of person who is always right, who tells his father he understands nothing because he is a poor peasant, who burns a little incense daily before the idol who has had the good fortune to be a "manager," a "boss," a "clerk," a "teacher," or, if I am a woman, a "beautiful body."

Then I remember the words of Jesus: "If you want to avoid judgment, stop passing judgment. Your verdict on others will be the verdict passed on you. The measure with which you measure will be used to measure you" (Matt. 7:1-2).

No, there is nothing wrong about debating the Church when we love her; it is wrong to debate her as outsiders, like a pure elite. No, it is not wrong to debate sin and the ugly things we see; it is wrong to pin them on to others and believe ourselves innocent, poor, and meek.

That is wrong.

Today people say, "The Church must be credible"; this statement lends itself to endless discussion.

Credible to whom? To someone who does not even believe in God? Impossible! The Church is incomprehensible to anyone looking at her through a window.

To someone who does not believe in Christ? Absurd! The mystery of the Church is the same as the mystery of Jesus. If one does not believe in the one, he cannot believe in the other.

To someone who believes that Jesus is the Son of God? Well then, yes.

The Church is credible to those who believe in

Jesus, because it is His own Church, His own continuation, His own fullness.

But the reasons for credibility are not the virtues of bishops nor the goodness of Christians nor the political positions Christians assume. The Church's credibility is in the fact that, notwithstanding two thousand years of sins committed by her personnel, she has preserved the faith, that this morning I saw one of her priests say over the bread, "This is my Body," and I received the Holy Communion of my master, the Lord Jesus.

Her credibility is in the fact that, ourselves notwithstanding, after twenty centuries of struggle, division, temptation, we are still a living body, and a society of prayer and grace, that today we feel as dramatic reality and authentic anchorage those words of Jesus: "the jaws of death shall not prevail against it" (Matt. 16:18).

The reason for credibility is that the passion of Christ continues here on earth through His saints, through His martyrs, through Christians who, although imperfect, really love Christ and are united to Him, and are one with Him. And they find in this mystery of the Church the only environment able to preserve the divine master and hear Him live through His words.

This is a mystery; it is a fact.

I accept the fact that the reality of the Church, the person of the Church, is wrapped round, like the Eucharist, in a veil of shadows which can only be reached by faith. But today I feel I must say what Peter said after the speech of Jesus on the bread of life—a speech which had thrown everyone into crisis and caused several to leave the group. This I must direct towards the Church, my Church, the Church of

Paul VI: "Lord, to whom shall we go? You have the words of eternal life" (John 6:68).

No, it is not rocks we must examine when we are thinking of the Chruch, whether it be the rock of Peter, the rock of James, the rock of Paul.

What we must examine is the promise of Jesus about her: "On this rock I will build my Church," and, even more, the person who, in the name of Jesus and the Father, can make separated things one—the Holy Spirit.

The mystery of the Church is the same mystery as that of the Holy Spirit: the uncreated love which unites Father and Son, and which unites us to God in Christ, after being poured out upon us at Pentecost.

The Holy Spirit is God's smile on mankind washed in the blood of Jesus; it is like His confidence, His trust in our attention. God, in the Holy Spirit, looks at mankind with a gaze of love and gives mankind the possibility of union with Him and, in Him, of union with our brothers.

The Holy Spirit, which is the same Spirit of Jesus and of the Father, is God's feast, God's joy, God's bliss, God's creativity, God's finger on our wounds, God's light in our hearts, God's mercy on our sins. The Holy Spirit is what happened to Zacchaeus as Jesus went by: "I give half my belongings, Lord, to the poor. If I have defrauded anyone in the least, I pay him back fourfold" (Luke 19:8). He is what passed in the heart of the Magdalene touched by Jesus; what illumined the intelligence of Peter under the action of the Father, and made him say: "You are the Messiah . . . the Son of the living God!" (Matt. 16:16).

What is the use of still looking at misdeeds of Zaccheus, at sins of Magdalene, at the weaknesses of Peter?

They are all part of the Church, as I am part of the Church, as those to be converted are part of the Church, as, potentially, the thief in a little Palestinian village, waiting for Jesus beside Him on Calvary is already part of the Church. Yes, the thieves, too, belong to the Church, and the overbearing, the exploiters, the capitalists; in other words, they are like the sick to be healed, the possessed to be liberated, the blind to be saved, the dead to be raised.

And they belong to the Church, not because I like them or do not like them, because they think as I do or disagree with me. They belong to the Church because God's gaze of love, which is the Holy Spirit, trusts them and wants to save them.

A union man with a Catholic background said to me, "I don't go to Mass in my parish any longer. The Eucharistic assembly seems false to me because my boss is beside me and I'm fighting against him in the trades union with all my might. I can't take communion with him."

There is the mistake. There is the point to which many Christians have come, often without their realizing it.

"I can't take communion with my enemy because I want to beat him."

What is left of the true gospel in this wrestlers' attitude?

What difference remains between Marx and Christ if I no longer take communion with my father's assassin? With someone who hates me? With someone who exploits me? Did not Jesus say, "Love your enemies and do good to those who hate you?" What will become of the Christian community when it makes class struggle its own method of freeing the oppressed?

Let us remember well: if I am not capable of pardoning those who wrong me, God will not pardon my wrongdoing. (Look at the parable of the pitiless servant in Matthew).

If I am not capable of trusting in the conversion of my enemy, God will take back His trust, which is the Holy Spirit.

And without the Holy Spirit, what am I?

Here is the greatest mystery of the Church, which I renounce when I close my heart to my enemy brother and set myself up as a judge over the assembly of the people of God.

The mystery is here.

This medley of good and ill, greatness and misery, holiness and sin, which is the Church, at bottom is myself.

Even if none of us who are living, who are in the Church, can call ourselves "Church," because the person "Church" is greater than they are, each one of us feels with trembling and infinite joy that what passes in the relationship of God-Church is something which belongs to his most intimate life.

In each one of us is reflected the threats and the sweetness with which God treats His people Israel, the Church. To each one of us God says, as to the Church: "I will espouse you to me forever" (Hos. 2:21). But at the same time he reminds us of our reality: "Yet not even with fire will its great rust be removed. Because you have sullied yourself with lewdness when I would have purified you, and you refused to be purified of your own uncleanness, therefore you shall not be purified until I wreak my fury on you" (Ezek. 12:12-13). It is enough to read the prophets to perceive how everything that God addresses to His people, to Israel, He says to each one of us.

And if the threats are so numerous and the violence of His punishment so great, even more numerous are His words of love and even greater is His mercy. God is greater than our weakness.

But there is another thing, perhaps the most beautiful. The Holy Spirit, who is love, is capable of seeing us holy, immaculate, beautiful, even if we are dressed as rogues and adulterers.

The pardon of God, when it touches us, makes Zacchaeus, the tax collector, become transparent and Magdalene, the sinner, immaculate.

It is as though evil had not been able to touch the metaphysical depths of man. It is as though love had kept the soul from being sullied when it was far from love.

God says to each one of us in pardon: "With age-old love I have loved you; so I have kept my mercy toward you. Again I will restore you, and you shall be rebuilt, O virgin Israel" (Jer. 31:3-4).

There, He calls us "virgins," even when we are on our way back from the umpteenth prostitution of our bodies, spirits, and hearts.

In this, God is truly God; that is, He is the only one capable of "making things new."

For it does not matter to me that He makes a new

190

heaven and a new earth; it is more necessary that He should make our hearts new.

That is the work of Christ.

That is the divine environment of the Church.

Do you want to hinder this making hearts new by turning someone out of the assembly of the people of God?

Or do you want, by searching for another, safer place, to put yourself in danger of losing the Spirit?

CHAPTER XX

" 'Love one another, as I have loved you!' "
(John 15:12)

Charity is God's way of loving; it is God's love itself.

It is a person who is called Holy Spirit.

It is the love which unites the Father with the Son.

It is the love which penetrated us at Pentecost.

We are baptized no longer in water, but in the fire of the Holy Spirit—that is, in love.

He who possesses the Holy Spirit and listens to Him understands everything; he who does not possess Him and does not listen understands nothing.

Light and darkness in our spirits are formed by this Spirit.

When He came down upon the chaos this Spirit created the universe.

When He covered Mary of Nazareth with His shadow, the flesh of the woman became the flesh of the Son of God.

The incarnation is the fruit of the Holy Spirit and mankind living in Mary.

He who was born of this union was called Jesus.

Jesus is God living in the flesh of man.

That is why He is simultaneously son of man and Son of God.

What He does as son of man, He does as Son of God.

The two natures belong to one person alone, that of Jesus.

Jesus is God made man.

Jesus is God near me.

Jesus is my master.

What Jesus does is the norm, the truth.

For each one of us, His gospel should be the constant search for a way to live on this earth.

It is the only book we need to know by heart.

And it is the gospel of love.

" 'Love one another as I have loved you' " (John 15:12).

Here is the summary of everything.

I can no longer say I am incapable of loving, because He replies to me, "I gave you charity at Pentecost."

I can no longer insist: What is charity for me, how can I get to know it, because He will tell me, "Do as I did. Love as I loved."

And how did you love, Jesus?

"I loved by dying for you. You try, too, to die for your brother."

What does it mean, Jesus, to die for my brother? Must I, too, expect an end like yours?

"No, I don't believe so and I hope not, because, although it is good to die crucified, it is not good that there should be crucifiers. Now I shall explain what dying for your brother means. Listen! 'Love you enemies, do good to those who hate you;' (Luke 6:27).

" 'When someone slaps you on one cheek, turn and give him the other;' (Luke 6:29).

" 'Be compassionate as your Father is compassionate' (Luke 6:36).

" 'Do not judge . . . Do not condemn . . . Pardon . . .' (Luke 6:37).

" 'Why look at the speck in your brother's eye, when you miss the plank in your own?' (Luke 6:41).

" 'Anyone among you who aspires to greatness must serve the rest' (Matt. 20:27)."

Enough, Jesus, quite enough. I am in the habit of forgetting these words. I should like you to explain to me through a simple example.

"Well, read over the story of the prodigal son: I am the father who pardons.

"If the same thing happens to you, act in the same way towards your son. It is a way of dying for one's son."

Another parable.

"Remember what happened on the road to Jericho, when the bandits assaulted a merchant and left him half-dead along the road?

"Don't act as those who shun the injured on the highway for fear of dirtying their car with blood, or of losing time. Stop and pick up your brother. It is a way of dying a little for him."

Another.

"Remember the parable of the servant whom his master had forgiven the enormous debt of ten thousand talents, $10,000, and the servant himself was incapable of forgiving his friend a little debt of a few dollars?

"Don't do that. You try, too, to forget your friends' debts, and so . . . you will learn to die a little for them."

Another one, lived by you, Jesus; a fact, not a parable.

"I had chosen Judas, like all the others, for that matter. But there was something wrong. No matter how many efforts I made, he did not and could not enter into the mystery of the kingdom, the demands of the good news.

"I knew that he was going to betray Me, that he was going to turn against Me. Already after the discourse at Caperneum on the Eucharist, I understood that he had set out on that road.

"And yet . . .

"And yet I bore with him, like all the others, as though everything were all right. I went on loving him . . .

"I tell you, he himself had offered Me occasion to get rid of him. He had started stealing from the common purse. I had proof several times. A little denouncement would have been enough; he would have been arrested and I should have been free of him.

"I did not say anything to him. I believe a man must be left free in his choices all the way to the end. This is the opinion of My Father, who has never blocked sinners, even when He could have. My Father is extremely sensitive to the freedom of each man.

"And I, too, was sensitive to the freedom of betraying Me, which my brother Judas had in his hands. And he betrayed Me.

"When he came to accompany the temple guards to my quarters, which he knew of, I still accepted his embrace, even though it was tied to the agony of being betrayed with a kiss.

"I should like My disciples to understand that the kingdom we are building together is different from all the other kingdoms, precisely because it is a kingdom of true love, not false love.

"And true love is rare, extremely difficult to live out.

"Look, it is a question of dying ourselves, not of making others die. It is too easy to thrust the spear into the hearts of others; it is much more difficult to thrust it into our own. And yet this is my revolution.

"And that is why I freely accepted the mounting of Calvary.

"Do you believe I could not have set myself free? It would have taken so little. No, I did not want to hold out hope to those who see the good news as the constitution of an ideal earthly kingdom, even if it were a kingdom of which I myself were king.

"It is always the same illusions that beguile the hearts of men: to reign, to dominate, to be strong, to be well, to have no need of anything or anybody, never to get ill, never to die, always to win.

"And at the end they are always surprised by reality, which is something different. The reality is that 'My Kingdom does not belong to this world' (John 18:36).

"The reality is that there is a passage, to which death is the door.

"The reality is that the resurrection cannot come about without death preceding it.

"My friends forget this too easily, but that is how it is!

"And it is not just a question of that death which is the final act of human life, but that death which I have shaped and which must be accepted every day in order to rise every day.

"After my death on Calvary, the sons of the kingdom were dead with Me, buried in My death; after My resurrection they arose with Me. But since I have not separated the two times, the two realities, they cannot, must not, separate the two mysteries.

"It is too easy to exalt oneself in My resurrection; it is too cheap not to want to pass through my death, even if it is costly.

"That is why it is difficult to love: man wants to rise without dying first.

"If lovers are not ready to die for one another, then love is soon consumed, withered, vanished.

"If man is ready to die for his brother, then love for his brother grows, lives to its fullness, and becomes eternal.

"He who loves must be ready to die.

"That is what I did, and I died for you.

"And My love for you is eternal, invincible.

"Do as I did, love as I loved, and you will know what the beatitude means. Remember that one act of mercy is worth more than one act of cunning, and that the diplomacy you put into your relationships is straw thrown to the wind.

"And do not forget that it is better to lose than to win, when to lose means to be humiliated before our brother.

"Do you want the secret of running swiftly on the road of love, of enjoying a great peace of heart? Here it is.

—Seek the last place before him whom you love.

—Lower yourself voluntarily, as I lowered Myself,

even though I was God. Concern yourselves with loving, not being loved.

—Do not look for human glory, but for the service of men.

—Do not go in for victimizing which eats your heart out, but be happy to be a joyous hidden victim.

—Do not believe in armed violence, not even the revolution; believe in the violence of love.

—Do not worry about converting the world; worry about converting yourselves.

—The smaller and poorer you are, the happier you will be.

When love crucifies you, remember I am near you."

CHAPTER XXI

" 'Live on in my love' " (John 15:9)

Jesus, it is so good to hear you speaking; speak to me again!

"What do you want me to tell you?"

You gave me the law of love, your love, and you made me understand that You are the law, You are the holy gospel, You are the way to love.

Help me, Jesus, to trace Your footsteps. It is so difficult! Don't leave me alone!

"Why do you say to me, 'Don't leave me alone'? I never leave you alone; I cannot, since I am within you."

It seems like a set phrase, Jesus, "You within me!, one of the rhetorical phrases which we use. But does it correspond to the truth, the whole truth?

Are You truly, effectively within me?

What mystery is in Your words, Jesus!"

"Yes, brother, I am within you.

"What would have been the use of my death, offered for love of you all, if not to carry out the reality of this union of ours?

"I died in order to overcome separation and to establish a kingdom in which *whoever wants to be with Me is with Me.*

"I have no difficulty in being with you because I love you seriously. It is you who sometimes escape from Me and try to stay far from Me.

"Isn't that how it is?"

Yes, it is true, Jesus, and I understand more and more the words you said at the Last Supper: "He who loves Me will be loved by my Father. I too will love him and reveal myself to him" (John 14:21).

To have You show Yourself to me, I must love You: that is the rule.

Isn't that how it is?

"Go ahead in the same Gospel of St. John and what do you find?"

" 'Anyone who loves Me

will be true to My word,

And My father will love him;

we will come to him

and make our dwelling place with him.' "

(John 14:23)

"There, John has not forgotten what I said on that evening, which was so beautiful and so terrible, the evening of the Supper.

"We will make our dwelling place with him. My Father and I dwell in men who believe and hear my word."

199

But how can this come about, Jesus?

You left the earth then; You died, You rose, You ascended into heaven?

"Read what John said. He was the one who was the most attentive to this thought: 'I will not leave you orphaned; I will come back to you' (John 14, 18). I am not in the habit of joking; the things I am telling you are true.

"If I told you, 'I will come back to you,' it is because I wanted to return to you, and to stay with you, to be with you.

"This was the plan of salvation followed since the beginning of the world.

"This is the kingdom, 'you in Me and I in you.' My death has broken the separations. That is why I have told you, 'The reign of God is already in your midst' (Luke 17:21).

"You go on like children, searching for heaven near the moon or the stars. But to see it, feel it, live it, you must look within yourselves. I, the king, am within you, and together we form the reign of God, which is something that *already exists,* even if it has yet to be made visible and proclaimed to all creation."

And how are You in me, Jesus?

How have You returned to me?

"Leaving the world with death, I returned to you with the Holy Spirit, which is the Spirit of the Father and My Spirit, which love makes one thing only.

"The holy Spirit is the love of God within you; that is why I have told you, 'you are inhabited by God.' "

How beautiful all this is, Jesus. Let me never forget it.

Let me live always conscious of Your presence

within me, which is the presence of the Father Himself. Let me be encouraged always by Your words: "Live on in my love" (John 15:9).

There. To be able to live in Your love, Jesus! To do everything in Your love. Here, I think, is the most precious key to existence, the most authentic summary of being Christians—beings shaped by You, carrying You, buried with You, risen with You, already in glory with You.

"But do you know why you are always making mistakes? Why you are always finding yourselves at the beginning again? Why you live in fear and constant lack of decision?

"Because you do not believe in this reality. Because you take those words, I in you and you in Me, to be rhetorical, whereas they are the naked truth.

"I am truly in you, I live in you, and you never realize it.

"It is rare to see you motionless before Me within you for one moment!

"You are so illogical!

"Why do you become so agitated? Why do you talk so much?

"You do everything except the most important thing: coming to find me within yourselves, standing to listen in peace and silence.

"I would teach you what to do. But you are too convinced that you already know what to do, and you behave as though I did not exist.

"One of the phrases you have forgotten most, which is just the one you ought to have remembered, is 'Without Me you can do nothing.' Oh, I did not mean to say that without Me you could not make aeroplanes or bake bread. 'I meant that without Me, who am the door, you could not enter the kingdom. Without Me, who am the light, you could not see my Father's affairs. Without Me, who am life, you could do nothing vital in the invisible Kingdom I founded.' "

What is it, Jesus, that most offends You in us, who have wanted to follow You?

"What offends Me most is your unbelief. You take the gospel as a fairy tale, or nearly so. You do not believe what I have said. If you believed you would know that I am within you as a living reality, not a beautiful, sentimental phrase. If you believed that I am within you, if you acted on my words 'Live on in my love,' all your problems would be resolved, and you would be Christians who were a bit more serious and less strange.

"You go to pray when you should be busy, and you bustle about when you should be stopping to think, to pray.

"You never reach the mean because you do not see and you cannot see without Me.

"You often make prayer itself into an idol, a kind of institution, something rhetorical and empty of sense, something that must be done because it is the rule. If you called yourself into My presence within you, which is the presence of love itself; if you brought yourself into the depths of your being, where I dwell; if you placed yourselves beside Me, as Mary did, to listen, oh, then you would know what prayer is, and you could no longer get on without it, just as I cannot get on without staying with the Father.

"*You in me, as I am in the Father, where we are consumed in unity.*

"That is truly love!

202

"If we speak of action, then your error is endless. You act as though everything depended on you; you bustle about as though creativity were within you. In the apostolate, you behave like creators, which you are not, you cannot be.

"There is only one creator: God.

"This is where you make your error and constantly go back to the beginning.

"This gives birth to all your fears, because fear is the fruit of your autonomy.

"It is one of your sufferings in the Church today, especially among the 'strong spirits,' among the 'great ones.' They are afraid that everything is crumbling, that everything is finished.

"This happens when, for too long, you have had faith in yourselves, faith in something created—even something good, even the Church.

"No, faith must be in God alone, who may claim it because He is God.

"If faith depended on men and their clairvoyance or ability, the Church would have been demolished by the first dispute in Jerusalem itself.

"You have no idea how many times in her history the Church would have been reduced to ashes if all had not been sustained by the presence of the Spirit which is in her.

"Oh, if the popes had always prayed!

"Oh, if the bishops would pray, and especially the priests, who are in close contact with the true frontier of good and evil, which is men! How easy everything would be!

"Then I should teach them everything, then I should

unveil the secrets of hearts and history! Then I should know how to console them!

"But praying does not mean staying on one's knees or one's feet, pronouncing formulas or celebrating rites. Praying means believing deep down in your own weakness and believing deep down in God's omnipotence.

"Praying means hoping in the promise contained in the whole history of salvation, not in the power of organization or the cunning of men.

"Praying means loving and doing everything because of love, not lining up for rites which often end as mere rhetoric when they are not animated by a decision of the will to do only the will of God.

"Oh, if Christians would pray! How different they would be from pagans, how the world would recognize them.

"And instead? What difference is there between one and the other?

"Above all, why do they no longer know how to express joy?

"This is grave, because the message of salvation, if it is salvation, is joy, exultation.

"Why is the Church so sad?

"Why is the priesthood so boring that it even has to ask itself the nature of its identity and the reasons for its existence?

"There is only one reply. In practice—not in theory—'They have forsaken Me, the source of living waters;/ they have dug themselves cisterns,/ broken cisterns, that hold no water' (Jer. 2:13).

"Oh, return to Me—the prophet would say—and put Me to the test: 'Shall I not open for you the floodgates

204

of heaven to pour down blessing upon you without measure' (Mal. 3:10)? For 'Is My hand too short to ransom' (Isa. 50:2)? Have I become incapable of helping you?"

"You will live in my love if you keep my commandments, even as I have kept my Father's commandments, and live in His love" (John 15:10).

"Leave your idols, which cannot help you.

"Do not believe in the strength of money, do not rely on the powerful. Rely on Me, who am God.

"Live on in my love," and rest in peace. " 'I have overcome the world' (John 16:33).

"Do not place yourselves with that world that I have overcome, which is power, money, sensuality, a world that I shall crush because it is a damned thing 'under the evil one' (1 John 5:19), a world for which I do not pray. (cf. John 17:9).

"Do not begin the day by reading the newspaper; that will make you slaves of public opinion, even though involuntarily. Rather, begin your daily labors waiting for the dawn in prayer, as the Psalm suggests to you: 'Awake, O my soul; awake, lyre and harp; I will wake the dawn' (Ps. 108:3). All those who have signed the story of my presence in the world have done so.

"Come to me, all you who are weary and find life burdensome, and I will refresh you. Take my yoke upon your shoulders and learn from Me, for I am gentle and humble of heart. Your souls will find rest . . ." (Matt. 11, 28-19).

"And in order to come to Me, you do not need to walk, because I am within you, at your center, in the most hidden place within you. That is Heaven, My Heaven and your Heaven. That is the meeting place between you and Me, between you and the Father in the Spirit, who, as He makes unity of our trinity, makes unity with you."

CHAPTER XXII

"Rejoice, O highly favored daughter! The Lord is with you." (Luke 1:28)

Jesus, I dare to ask you one thing: speak to me about Your mother. When I look at her, I feel I am unable even to think.

When I was small, my mother used to make me say the rosary. This practice still was common in the Church, and, even if it was a prayer that made me go off to sleep, it filled my heart with so much peace, I felt satisfied, truly satisfied.

Then came the time in which we learnt "to think." We no longer went off to sleep while we said our prayers, but the satisfaction, the peace, the joy disappeared.

Above all, she disappeared—Your mother.

How many of us no longer feel her near us, no longer know what to say to her. Some people are even afraid to introduce her into their relationship with You, as though there were some element of exaggeration, of sentimentality, of something less serious.

Not to mention those who speak coldly about her, those who are motivated only by the fear that if they do not speak about Your mother, they are not good Christians!

I believe there are few themes on which there has been so much rhetoric as on the theme of Your mother.

Is that not so?

Well, I would like you to speak to me about her, to tell me if she is with us as she was with You, as mother; if she comes close to us as she came close to You, when You were tiny and needed her.

"Well, yes, let us begin by speaking about why you feel her less close. Why you have so much difficulty reciting the rosary. Why you get bored with this prayer, so simple and childlike and tiny, and yet so profound and contemplative.

"You have become too intellectual, too cunning. By now you have become more followers of Descartes than sons of hers.

"Oh, let's understand each other.

"It is not wrong to use intelligence or reasoning in scientific research: it is the most suitable instrument.

"It is not wrong to be dominated by reason in all that pertains to the visible. It is wrong to pretend to understand the mysteries of God or to pierce the invisible with that instrument.

"After so many centuries, you always return to the same point: confusing reason with faith, wanting to use something limited—such as human reason—to penetrate heaven.

"Faith has the dimensions of God, reason has the dimensions of man.

"Faith opens the secrets of heaven, reason opens those of the earth.

"Faith takes you into My presence, reason leads you into the presence of things.

"If reason could penetrate Heaven, how could the little ones, who have such a small supply, come to Me?

"Even my mother would not have been able to come to Me. She was a housewife, simple, like the women of her time. She did not know whether the earth was round or flat.

"No, it is not reason that can penetrate heaven, that can understand the invisible, that can stand in contemplation before Me; it is only faith.

"And it is faith that helped my mother, sustained my mother, made her answer 'yes' even when she could not understand. Even when, by accepting My request, she faced no small difficulties.

"That is why you do not feel my mother near you: because you are not on the same wave length. You are afraid of living on faith, so you try to resolve your relationships with God by the pale light of your reasoning.

"And naturally you find the door closed.

"My mother was a woman of faith, and it is on this road that she can be your mother and your teacher.

"Try to put yourself in her place, if you want to understand at what point she succeeded in supporting the encounter between faith and reason, between the visible and the invisible, between what can be understood and what must be believed. Try to think what happened to her.

"Hearing from the angel that she was to become

mother of the Son of God might have been something intriguing; but not being able to explain her condition to Joseph, who was her fiancé and who absolutely could not grasp the significance of the mystery which was being fulfilled within her, was not so intriguing!

"Seeing some flash of light over the cave of Bethlehem may have given her a certain comfort, but realizing that Herod's soldiers were about to slay all the Messiah's little companions of misfortune was not something very acceptable to reason.

"Feeling My intimacy, sharing My vocation to its depths, bearing the cry of the crowd that wanted Me dead were not easy for her.

"Having a dead body between her hands on Calvary, on that tragic Friday, and believing in My Resurrection was not the reasoning of this world.

"And so on right up to the end, My mother lived on pure faith, and God's love for her did not spare her sufferings so atrocious that it is difficult to imagine their extent.

"If she gave birth to Me without sorrow in Bethlehem, the Church was not born in the same way. The cost of Calvary and the lack of understanding on the part of men—all men, including our most intimate friends—made her truly deserve the title of Mother of the Church.

"And she always walked in faith, dark as the night, until the end of her bitter road, until My embrace after her passage.

"Only then could she breathe, since her struggle in the spirit was so harsh as to have no equal in any other creature of earth.

"But there is another thing my mother can teach you: *to live.*

"And here we return to the central defect of your time. The sons of Descartes have caused it, and because of it you no longer understand the closeness of my mother, who is too different from you!

"You turn the gospel, the message of salvation, into an idea. You live on ideas, you feed on ideas, you are interested in ideas, you fill the day with ideas.

"And do you not know that I came to bring not an idea, but a life—the life?

"What relationship can you still have with my mother, who had no ideas at all?

"But she lived.

"I was her life.

"Her womb did not carry an idea; it carried Me, who am the Life.

"And the life developed in quite a special way: it is the fruit of love, not problems; struggle and blood, not words.

"It is no longer possible to come into a group of your militants without hearing words, words, words.

"How can you understand my mother, who never spoke?

"The difference between words and life, between chattering and life, is the difference between being and nothing, between making love and talking about love, between praying and speaking about prayer, between eating and talking about bread.

"You talk instead of eating, you discuss instead of praying, you speak of love instead of being love.

"My mother did just the opposite. She prayed, she

was silent, she loved, and, in that way, divine life developed within her.

"But then there was something in her that you have completely lost.

"She did not speak about Me, but looked at Me. She did not study theology, but listened, even to my breathing during the night. She did not consider herself a missionary, but 'kept all these things in memory' (Luke 2:51).

"And you? You talk about Me constantly without knowing Me; you pour over theology books for hours and hours without wanting to stay with Me a while in silence, in a church; you want to save the Third World and you fail to put a little salvation into your disordered hearts, which, are without peace and without joy.

"If you would search for divine life, which is 'I in you' (John 14:20), you would meet My mother, who did nothing but carry within herself divine life in order to give it to the world. I was her heaven, I was her intimacy, I was her contemplation, I was her inspiration, I was her action.

"And I was enough for her!

"She was happy, even if the sword of her divine maternity pierced her heart constantly.

"She did not believe that she was the builder of history, as you do; she lived in her smallness and attributed to God—and God only—the possibility of guiding things.

"She believed herself to be nothing before God, so she never wanted to mirror herself in her own responsibility, as you do.

"Yes, you are afraid of what history will say about

212

you, and it is your limitless pride which makes you think this way.

"She did not have this fear, and in her simplicity she lived day by day, as the poor of the earth live, the real poor, those who know they count for nothing in the balance of events.

"Do you want proof of the difference between your constant worry and the freedom of my mother in her extraordinary humility of life?

"One day, during a pilgrimage to Jerusalem I hid, and she mislaid Me.

"Have you mislaid Me?

"No, you have not mislaid Me.

"So as not to lose Me, so that history would not call you a distracted people, you have tied Me to your arms with a rope, and you have not left Me the least Freedom.

"My mother was capable even of mislaying Me, so free was she in her immense humility.

"It was this humility of her, this smallness of hers, this lack of self-regard, this not valuing herself for anything, that made Me love her.

"No other creature was so capable of humility as my mother!

"And this is her greatness before God!

"There is why you do not feel my mother close to you. You will not be able to feel her until you have changed your hearts.

"My mother is the model of life and of humility; you are models of big words and vanity.

"My mother is the mistress of faith and total abandonment to God; you are models of frozen rationality and constant inconsistencies.

"My mother was poor and free as a bird in the sky; you are rich and slaves of your presumed culture and your sad, poisoned comfort."

"But let us come to the secret of her being.

"What was My mother?

"What did My mother inaugurate?

"What did My mother live?

"It was the kingdom of God.

"She inaugurated the kingdom of God on earth.

"She lived the kingdom of God.

"For the first time in time, the eternal desire of God to live under the tents of men was fulfilled in her.

"Mary was the first tent under which the Absolute lived as though in His own home, conversing with men, living in peace with men.

"Always Yahweh had had the desire of setting up His tent among men. To live with them in perfect union, to establish with them an ideal kingdom of peace, where war would be banished and happiness would be at home.

"He had never succeeded.

"No creature had ever accepted becoming God's tent, absolutely under His domination.

"Too many idols filled up the space of their freedom.

"The first creature who knew how to say and wanted to say her unconditional yes to God's desire was My mother: 'I am the servant of the Lord. Let it be done to me as you say' (Luke 1:38).

"It was the first time that God had heard such a sweet word from men. Everyone had only worried about questions and denials, as though the kingdom of God were less interesting than the kingdom of the earth, as though living with men were more pleasing than living with God.

"My mother was capable of an absolute act of abandonment, of radical humility, and of a perfect vision of reality.

"And she conceived Me.

"I lived in her womb as in Paradise, at my ease.

"My mother's womb was truly a piece of Heaven. It was Heaven.

"In her, God's dream was realized: to make a heaven of earth, 'on earth as it is in heaven' (Matt. 6:10)!

"Do you want to become heaven?

"Do as My mother did: accept Me to dwell with you.

"Do you want to become God's tent? Accept Me within you, as My mother did.

"Here is the summary of the whole plan of salvation; here is God's secret; here is the sign of His infinite mercy; here is the greatness of the human vocation. To be God's dwelling place yourselves, to live union with the eternal, to make heaven in man, to make the kingdom of the Creator out of a creature.

"My mother is the origin of all this; she inaugurated this divine reality in her flesh.

"Whoever wants to enter this divine reality must follow her.

"That is how My mother is your mother.

"Accept her and you will be holy, because holiness is nothing more than God dwelling within you and the conscious acceptance of being the dwelling place of God. That is what my mother did fully.

"Then you will understand everything, for your understanding will come from within, as a fruit of life and as a reply to intimacy with the eternal truth of God.

Then you will be in peace, because peace is the fruit of the order I have established between Heaven (which is God) and the earth (which is you).

"Nothing will ever be able to make you afraid again, since you carry God Himself and His omnipotence within yourselves.

"Nothing will ever be able to upset you again, since, being God's Heaven, you already have the kingdom within yourselves, unfailing and eternal, established since time began and forever by My Father."

"One more thing my mother can teach you, a precious thing in these secular and difficult times: the strength to suffer lovingly.

"In her such strength was limitless and came from her vocation to generate life.

"Oh, it is not easy to generate life in a land of death, to generate life in an inhospitable desert, such as the heart of sinful man. What anguish, to be faced with the horrible chaos of a man dominated by the demons of power, money, libido.

"How can such terrestrial reality be transformed into Heaven, such refined selfishness into generosity, such total slavery into freedom?

"There is little that can be done: it is necessary to suffer, suffer a great deal, as mothers suffer for their ungrateful sons, as the innocents suffer for those who trample them, as the poor suffer for those who starve them.

"It is necessary to have a great ability to suffer, so as not to fall into the temptation of hatred and not to accumulate, through violence, more dead bodies on the mountain already piled high.

"For if the mother rebels, perhaps without understanding, in front of her sinful son, who is to save him?

"If the innocent strikes out at the one who has struck him, who is to stop the spiral of violence?

"If the poor man kills the master who despises him and starves him, who on earth will still be capable of being 'the poor man'?

"Don't you know that if you are not poor, you cannot enter into the kingdom?

"And don't you know that only 'poverty' is the path which leads to the life of God?

"And what is meant by poverty as a beatitude? As I said in the Sermon on the Mount: 'How blest are the poor in spirit: the reign of God is theirs' (Matt. 5:3). It is the loving, beatifying acceptance of one's own limits, one's own imprisonment, one's own sorrow, one's own infirmity, one's own death.

"Oh, do not reduce poverty to something material, do not reduce it to not having money.

"For man, poverty is his own human nature, his 'state,' his being.

"For man poverty is the thirst for life without yet possessing life, the search for the Absolute while still living in the contingent, the hunger for God while not yet being God, the hope of the Resurrection while still immersed in death.

"This is poverty: such a tension is the only basis for relationship between man and God.

"Without poverty, man could not march towards God because he would not feel the need. Worse, without poverty man would believe himself to be God, adoring himself in a diabolical idolatry like a prolonged, radical curse.

"Without poverty man would become Satan."

"That is exactly how it is!

"So as not to let you become Satan, God has made poverty the inheritance of the earth, the ground of your growth, the environment of your sanctification, the stimulus to your march forwards.

"You will repair the house on one side and a crack will open on the other.

"Seven fat seasons will enrich your granaries, and seven lean seasons will deplete the stores. You will recover from one illness, and you will feel latent within you the signs of another.

"You will run to the right to give a hand to your brother, and close behind you three more will fall down, preys to the poverty that your own love has failed to satisfy.

"You will dedicate yourself to a thousand good works, and you will feel incapable of getting your son to obey you or making peace with your wife.

"You will feel generous enough to save all men, and you will not succeed in freeing your heart from a love which is poisoning and debasing you.

"You will be applauded as a man of worth and given the vote to govern, and when you have barely come into power you will feel incapable of solving daily problems and grieve at not being able to do anything for someone who is waiting."

"This is poverty.
"And suffering is its price.
"But when the ability to suffer, to have patience, gushes from the vein of love like a fire, it forges in

218

man, little by little, a soldering between the visible and the invisible, between his weakness and God's omnipotence, between non-being and Being, between earth and Heaven.

"This soldering, made with the fire of sorrow on the cleft of man's poverty, becomes the meeting place, the bridge of passage, the terrain of the invisible kingdom of God.

"I would say more: it is the new heaven and the new earth promised in scripture and proclaimed by the hope of man.

"And it is beatitude, because it is affirmation of God's victory over the poverty and the weakness of His creature, and it is announcement of the resurrection over the tragedy of death.

"God meets man at the crossroads of his poverty, in the bowl of his hunger, in the thirst of his need, in the realization of his limits as a creature, in the agony of his death.

"And He meets him to give him what he is searching for.

"And He gives it to him, but no longer in its created form, but in the uncreated.

"No longer in images, but in reality.

"No longer in time, but in eternity.

"Thus the earthly home becomes the heavenly home.

"The bread of the earth becomes the bread of God.

"The health of the body, eternal salvation.

"The life of man, the eternal life of God."

CONCLUSION

During my life I have had plenty of time to discover my poverty in body, in heart, in spirit.

At first it anoyed me; sometimes it scandalized me, as something incomprehensible.

Then it made me think.

The meeting with Jesus in the gospel taught me endurance, resignation, acceptance of this poverty of mine.

But when He, Jesus, and the Father sent me the Holy Spirit, I understood and lived the beatitude of poverty—the loving and joyful understanding of my limits, the certainty that life is born of death, the contemplative experience that visible things are images of the invisible and that poverty on this earth is only thirst for heaven, which is thirst for the Absolute.

Then I walked with faith on the path of my poverty to meet with Him, the Invisible, the Eternal One, Life, Light, Love, the Merciful One, the Personal God, the God of Abraham, the God of Moses, the God of Elijah, the God of Jacob, the God of Christ.

The meeting has not always been easy: darkness, nausea, dryness, desire to escape.

But I have remained, sustained by hope.

I have understood that God is the God who comes.

And I have waited.

For me to pray means to wait.

On the frontier of my limits, in the tension of my love, to have the strength to wait.

He always came, even if His manner of coming was always new, because He is always new and He is eternal multiplicity, though in the infinite unity of His nature.

I tell you little when I say I have gotten on well with Him, though He has nearly always offered me a painful love, in the image and substance of Jesus crucified, and He has strongly invited me to identify my love with the sorrow of the whole world and the suffering of my brothers.

And I expect—if His grace sustains me, as I hope it will—to return every dawn and every evening of my life to that meeting place.

And even if I foresee that my poverty will grow as I approach death, and that the waiting will be always more bitter, I no longer wish to break the appointment.

By now the God who comes has conquered me, and my eyes, tired of seeing only things here below, are happy to smile at Him.

And I should like them to be well opened and ready to smile before His marvels when He comes the last time to break through the veil of my limits and to introduce me—with all "His people" which is the Church—into His invisible Kingdom of light, life, and love.

In order to hurry that day, from now on I am taking for myself the most beautiful prayer, expressed in the last words of Revelation and placed like a seal on revealed things:

"Come Lord Jesus."

How I embrace as mine the joyful hope contained in the reply:

"Yes, I am coming soon."

Amen!